THE WAY WE WERE

THE WAY WE WERE

New England Then, New England Now

Daniel Okrent *1945*

Grove Weidenfeld · New York

Published by Grove Weidenfeld
A Division of Wheatland Corporation
841 Broadway
New York, New York 10003-4793

Published in Canada by General Publishing Company, Ltd.

Portions of this book have appeared in *New England Monthly.*

Library of Congress Cataloging-in-Publication Data

Okrent, Daniel, 1948-
    The Way We Were: New England then, New England now / Daniel Okrent.—1st ed.
        p.   cm.
    ISBN 1-55584-358-1
    1. New England—Description and travel—1981-   2. New England—Description and
    travel—1865-1950.   3. New England—Social life and customs.   I. Title.
    F10.O38   1989
    974'.04—dc20   89-33243
                                                                             CIP

Manufactured in the United States of America

This book is printed on acid-free paper

Designed by Michael Grinley, and Hans Teensma of Impress

First Edition, 1989

10 9 8 7 6 5 4 3 2 1

To all my colleagues at *New England Monthly,*
and to Chris Jerome

Contents

Acknowledgments

L ET ME BE FRANK: the idea for this book was lifted nearly intact from my friend Nicholas Lemann — entirely, I'm happy to say, with his permission. It was in 1981 that Nick discovered the Standard Oil archive at the University of Louisville, which eventually led to the publication of his own book on the project, *Out of the Forties*. When Robert Nylen and I founded *New England Monthly* three years later, Nick urged me to take a trip to Louisville. There, he insisted, I'd find a trove of New England photographs as rich as any in the entire collection.

It took me a few years to get to Louisville, and even then I simply followed my colleague John Tayman. John, who was *New England Monthly*'s picture editor at the time, made the first pass through the voluminous Louisville archives. Moreover, his subsequent reporting and research greatly enhanced my understanding of the New England revealed in these pictures.

Other current and former *New England Monthly* colleagues have also contributed greatly to this project. Greg Lauzon and Ron A. Cesar Jr. did most of the caption research, and Lisa Stiepock and Claudine Pilon pitched in as well. Hans Teensma and Mike Grinley designed the book; Lisa Newman coordinated its preparation; Dick Todd both edited the article on which it was based and put in the extra hours at the magazine that enabled me to complete the book. Vivi Mannuzza fought her way valiantly through thickets of prose. Bob Nylen, who is *New England Monthly*'s publisher, was immensely patient, tolerant, and supportive throughout this book's gestation. It isn't easy to research and write a book while trying to put out a monthly magazine — unless, that is, your partner is Bob Nylen.

Among those not on the magazine's staff, I wish to thank Anne Lusk, Glenn Perry, Liz Darhansoff, and my editor at Grove Weidenfeld, Bill Strachan; Becky, John, and Lydia Okrent, who put up with me; and David Horvath, Bill Carner, James Anderson, and their colleagues at the Photographic Archive of the Ekstrom Library at the University of Louisville. These people preside over a wondrous facility, and their cooperative spirit is matched only by their expertise.

Finally, I would like to acknowledge three other groups of people: the wonderful photographers who created these pictures; the subjects who posed for them; and, most of all, everyone I interviewed during my travels through New England. I don't know how I'd react if a stranger appeared at my door bearing aged pictures of my neighbors and my relatives, but I hope I could display half the generosity that so many people showed me. They took me into their homes and into their lives, and if this book has any value at all it is because of them.

— D. O.
Worthington, Massachusetts
February 1989

New England Then, New England Now

New England Then,
New England Now

O N A GOLDEN OCTOBER morning in 1987, I set out in search of Sylvester and Janie Moore, the farm couple from Skowhegan, Maine, in the picture on the facing page. A freakish early snow had fallen the day before, and a few patches of white still dotted the rocks along I-91 as I headed north through the Connecticut Valley. In sheltered spots, the bright maples against the incongruous snow seemed like an overwrought calendar artist's version of New England. But by noon, by the time I reached Hanover, the temperature had reached the mid-sixties; by the time I got to the Maine–New Hampshire border on Route 2, it was summer again.

It was summer, too, when Gordon Parks spent several days with the Moores, forty-three years earlier. In 1944 Parks, who would later become one of *Life* magazine's most celebrated photographers, was then a young photojournalist on assignment for the Standard Oil Company of New Jersey — Esso at the time, Exxon today. Roy Stryker, the man Parks was working for, had been brought in by the oil giant's managers to improve the company's image. Under attack for suspected complicity with an arm

1. Hercules Brown
Somerville, Maine
(page 83)

2. Washington Square
Newport, Rhode Island
(page 87)

3. Poultry stand, Augusta, Maine
(page 127)

4. Canadian Pacific Railway
North Troy, Vermont
(page 169)

of the Nazi industrial machine, Esso had picked Stryker, a populist, left-wing scholar, to serve as the agent of its public relations salvation.

Earlier, Stryker had directed the Farm Security Administration's celebrated photography project in the 1930s. Asked by Esso to document the role of oil in the life of America by using the techniques he had perfected at the FSA, Stryker couldn't resist the opportunity to deploy the resources of the stoutest heir of the Rockefeller Trust. Surely Stryker knew that the people he intended to hire — Parks, Russell Lee, Esther Bubley, John Vachon among them, the best photojournalists of the day — would take their mandate broadly: they would simply shoot the life of the era, with or without the Esso sign in view.

The earliest of the pictures in the fat folder beside me on the car seat — a Maine country-store owner (1) — was dated January 1944; the latest, from 1956, showed a street scene in Newport, Rhode Island (2), when the U.S. Navy was the old resort town's liveliest presence. Although Stryker's photographers traveled throughout the country and to various Esso installations overseas, they covered New England especially well. Together, the New England pictures revealed America at the last moment before television, before suburbanization, before the enormous democratizing force of the GI Bill was fully felt. In New England, Stryker's team of photographers saw the past just as the future had reached the doorstep.

Most of the people in the photographs would be dead now, I realized. Of the rest, all but the young children would be at least edging into old age. I hoped that by talking to a few of these people, and others who knew them, I might learn about our great leap forward into the modern age, what it had done for us and what it had cost us. On that bright October day, I hoped to discover something about who we are, and how we got here, and what four decades had done to a life that appeared in the photographs as distant, and as alluring, as history itself.

One could argue that the New England pictures slice so deep into the soul because of the special place that these six states occupy in the national mythology. New England is the imagined home of every American; you do not survive a lifetime's exposure to such icons as the saga of the Revolution, the steepled country church, or the tidy village of hardy yeomen without a sense of affinity branded into your consciousness. The

New England landscape, so distinct to this corner of the country, is paradoxically universal.

And what a landscape it was! The Maine farm woman in front of her roadside stand (3), the muscular steam locomotive chugging off for Canada (4), the Vermont children celebrating the end of school (5), the rural Connecticut tableau (6); each confirms that the images of fondest recollection were painted from life. Back in the 1940s, major highways led through town centers, farmers were near their markets, businessmen on their lunch hours could buy the afternoon newspaper from the boy — however old he was, he was always a boy — who stood on the street corner day after day. In the evenings, families like the Thibodeaus of Lancaster, New Hampshire, gathered around the radio, or spent the hours before bedtime reading.

Downtowns were thriving then. Ryan Drug, on Main Street in Springfield, Massachusetts (7), had just written its one millionth prescription. There were no malls, at least not until Shoppers World, in Framingham, Massachusetts (8), opened in 1951. Public transportation was as firm a fact of city life as pavement itself, and trolley tracks bisected the main streets of towns throughout the region. Agricultural fairs were everywhere, economic engine for the farmers, diversion for nearby town dwellers. The family farm remained the primary unit of American food production. Most cities still encouraged industrial development; just outside Boston, in Everett, Massachusetts, where Esso operated the only oil refinery in New England, the citizens of the town liked to brag about having more of its square miles in heavy industry than any other city on the Eastern Seaboard. Industry meant jobs — what *sort* of job barely mattered for a largely undereducated population. New England made things then, made shoes and textiles, grew cauliflower and turnips, fashioned clapboards for sturdy, foursquare homes. Schools were good, people went to church, they cared about their neighbors.

Such were the people I was looking for when I arrived in Skowhegan — the family farmer, the brawny tradesman happy in his work, the hearthside group sharing a moment in the gentle evening. What the pictures in the file folder showed, I thought, was authenticity: real people living real lives, uncorrupted by the thin promises of our own media-saturated age.

5. Schoolhouse
East Roxbury, Vermont
(page 122)

6. Feed store
Suffield, Connecticut
(page 166)

7. Ryan Drug
Springfield, Massachusetts
(page 97)

8. Shoppers World
Framingham, Massachusetts
(page 79)

The forms of life still conformed to life's functions. Scythes were used to cut grass, not as ornaments to hang over a garage door. Before television created its daily depictions of Ozzies and Harriets (much less Blakes and Krystles), people weren't constantly assaulted by reminders of some imagined, better life, where work barely existed and domestic amity was as natural as sunshine. Life for most Americans was the thing you lived, not the envy-making daydream offered in a relentless, commerce-driven bombardment that a later generation could not escape. There was, in the Esso pictures, an uncompromised honesty to New England life, and I wanted to learn what had happened to it.

Once in Skowhegan, a town of 8,000 in west central Maine, it took me less than a day to begin to find tangible traces of the stolid farm couple, Sylvester and Janie Moore — models, almost, of my longed-for authenticity. By piecing together the paper trail of deeds, wills, and court records they had left behind, I was soon able to discern the outline of their lives; from talking to people who knew them, I learned what paper didn't tell. Finally, visiting the farm they and then their son Turney inhabited for more than four decades, I discovered how the life the Moores had known had come to its end.

How it started was itself remarkable. Sylvester Moore, who was born in New Brunswick in 1866, trekked south to Skowhegan with Janie, their younger children, and a herd of Ayrshires in 1920. The motives for his move are lost to time and faulty memories, but the impact was profound. For the Moore family, Sylvester's decision to rip up one life and begin another (he was already past fifty when he journeyed south) set in motion the machine of history: a vast, powerful centrifuge that, generation after generation, spins lives outward in ever widening arcs.

On arriving in Skowhegan, Sylvester bought 170 acres of Kennebec River bottomland for roughly $7,700. The Moores belonged to a loose community of New Brunswickers in the area, but, save for the occasional multifamily picnic, there would be hardly any evidence of leisure in Sylvester's life. No one ever knew Sylvester Moore to go fishing; he never took part in local politics; he kept to himself, a rather forbidding figure to children from the other farms on the River Road.

Among their neighbors and the other Skowhegan farmers, however, the Moores were considered something of an elite. Sylvester worked terribly hard and built up a large herd of cows, which he traded with the canniness of a land speculator. But by the time Gordon Parks came by in the summer of 1944, the seventy-eight-year-old Moore was presiding over a farm whose day-to-day operations had been placed in the hands of Turney Moore (9), the one son who had stayed by Sylvester's side.

Someone who knew the Moores well remembers a deathly chill that distanced Sylvester from his wife. Local rumor insisted that Janie had been his family's servant on their New Brunswick farm, and a surprise pregnancy had forced the marriage. One who had worked for the Moores in Skowhegan told me about the bottle of gin Sylvester kept secreted in the pantry, a bottle he marked with a line after his every drink so he would know whether anyone else had dipped into it. When he died, in 1949, Sylvester left $100 to each of his six children who were living away from Skowhegan and everything else to Janie. Turney, who had stayed home, would inherit the farm when Janie died, less than a year later. He was fifty.

But Turney Moore's patrimony was a flawed legacy, misshapen by family history and the larger forces of modernity's rush. Years earlier he had purchased the land adjoining his father's, and through the 1940s he had taken the operating responsibility for both farms. The two Moore men were set up in business as S. B. Moore and Son, the father clinging to his patriarchal authority and the son spreading his labor over the soil. If Turney wanted to buy a new piece of equipment, the old man would clutch his pocketbook in a death grip. Yet if the Moore land had any future at all, it was in Turney's hands. His formal education had ended when Sylvester yanked him out of the seventh grade to help chop turnips, but Turney didn't lack personal resources. "Turney was well respected by men," his brother-in-law, Ray McLaughlin, told me, "a real worker who could do anything." But because of his father's inability to see beyond the tidy, enclosed, and essentially cheerless world he had so painstakingly constructed, Turney's task was daunting.

9. Turney Moore
Skowhegan, Maine
(page 131)

When Sylvester died, Turney joined the two farms and invested in the equipment he needed. But by then, in the early 1950s, time had turned against him. Health regulations required dairy farmers to keep their milking machines in a separate barn, and soon the law mandated the use of costly,

10. Esso physician
Everett, Massachusetts
(page 119)

stainless-steel holding tanks for milk products. Modern methods of marketing had begun to make the independent farmer less important to the large dairy firms, and Turney's income could not keep up with his escalating costs.

History's move against Turney Moore, and against the small farm itself, had been hardly capricious; if anything, it was late in arriving. The health code protected the consumer from disease, and the efficiency of the large dairy marketers helped keep retail milk prices down. The tuberculosis examination conducted by the doctor in the photograph (10) would become a rarity as code changes pushed the bovine tubercle bacillus toward extinction. At the same time, the milk marketers were bringing a new efficiency to the distribution of dairy products. As long ago as the early 1950s, Melissa Giles, who owned the farm adjoining the Moores' with her late husband, Guy, would bring in extra cash selling homemade butter. Good as it was, her butter sold for a fifty percent premium over what the big dairies charged.

With the logic of the family farm bent out of shape by new realities, Turney Moore would in time find himself imprisoned by his long years of apprenticeship. For nearly unimpeachable reasons, the world would have increasingly little use for his kind of farm, and through the 1950s he was compelled to sell off house lots wherever he had road frontage, gathering the cash needed to keep his business alive. An ever growing tax burden — for roads, for schools, for cleaning up the effluents that had choked the Kennebec to within an inch of its life — led him to sell his home and move into a house trailer, occupying himself with occasional carpentry and logging work. His only son, John, had his eyes elsewhere; what allure could the grinding, losing battle of farming possibly hold for him? Now John had the chance to ride the centrifuge, a chance created first by his grandfather's move south from New Brunswick decades earlier, then forced into play by his father's struggles. It sent John spinning out toward alternatives, possibilities. He went off to Bowdoin College in 1957, eventually earned a Ph.D. in physics at the University of Illinois, and finally settled a continent away, in a suburb of Portland, Oregon. By then Turney, who knew how perspective could divide a father and his son, told a friend that he and John "can't even talk to each other. We're on totally different planes."

As I traveled out to the Moore place that October afternoon, it was hard to imagine that Sylvester and Janie's world was less than a lifetime distant. Electricity had reached that part of Skowhegan only ten years before Parks took his pictures. Today a gallery of housing styles, evidence of virtually every mass architectural trend from the 1950s to the 1980s, lines the River Road, many of them on lots Turney had once farmed. The fields that two generations of Moores had tamed have reverted to brush and tall grass. A few miles beyond the Moore farm, the immense main plant of the S. D. Warren paper company's Somerset division, built in 1976, blocks both sky and horizon. Satellite dishes grow along the roadside like some hyperfertilized crop.

But I discovered at least one fingerprint remained from the Moores' lives. At the large home that had once belonged to Turney, I met Reggie Perkins. A slender man in his fifties, Perkins had lived in Skowhegan as a boy and then had settled in Cape Elizabeth, near Portland. He liked living next to the Atlantic, but suburban life displeased him and he came back to Skowhegan in 1985, four years after Turney Moore's death. He told me about the upholstery business he runs from one of the farm's outbuildings, but I was more interested in the barn — Turney's old barn, identical to the one that served as the backdrop to Parks's portrait of his parents.

Perkins was happy to oblige my curiosity. Though he didn't farm, he was clearly proud of the old, brooding structure. We walked over to the barn, about a hundred yards from the river, and Perkins leaned into the door. As it creaked open, the sun raced in ahead of us. At once I saw the same loft, the same rusted hayfork in the picture of Sylvester and Janie — and there in the middle of the barn's emptiness, rising in perspective above us, an immense speedboat up on a trailer.

We walked back out into the autumn light, I a little dazed, Perkins talking about how he liked to cruise up and down the river. Then he pointed toward the land that stretched down to the bank, the sweep of his arm as expansive as I imagine Sylvester Moore's might have been had his prize Ayrshires been grazing before us. "I'm planning a pitch-and-putt course right here," Perkins said. He pointed to a rill that emptied into the Kennebec. "One of the holes will go ninety-five yards right down to the river, and you'll have to pitch over that creek to get to the green."

11. Harry Haas, West Springfield, Massachusetts
(page 65)

12. Center Street
Lyndonville, Vermont
(page 156)

13. Thibodeau family
Lancaster, New Hampshire
(page 60)

FOR THE TWO MONTHS that I continued my journeys around New England, the boat in the barn grew to be an all-purpose symbol: it simultaneously represented the debasement of Turney Moore's labors and the fruit of Reggie Perkins's, both the corrupting power of leisure and the pleasure that leisure can bring. Mostly, it signaled the end of authenticity, and authenticity's shortcomings.

"It was a wonderful life back then," Melissa Giles told me in the living room of her farmhouse, just up the road from the Moore place. She wore a blue cotton dress with a red bow at the collar, and her eyes glistened with the memories she shared with me: how the Giles family always ate together, three meals a day, seven days a week, the food pure and good; how neighbors helped neighbors. But then her daughter, Janice, a schoolteacher who lives with her, spoke up. Janice remembered those things the Esso pictures didn't reveal — the endless work and the empty pockets, a life with few material comforts, no vacations, limited choices. The only luxury the Gileses had, she said, was a washing machine, purchased with scrimped pennies. "It was a wonderful life," Melissa had said, but now Janice asked, "Did you really think so then, Mother?" Melissa didn't answer.

The boat in the barn: it could have been the endless stretch of tract homes blanketing the land in West Springfield, Massachusetts, that young Harry Haas plowed forty-four years ago (11); it could have been the Federal Express pickup box around the corner from where the young mother pushed her baby in a sled in Lyndonville, Vermont (12); it could have been the prospect of brighter horizons that led Gauthier Thibodeau, the man (13) reading the paper, to leave his wife and family in Lancaster, New Hampshire, marry another woman, and seek his fortune in Venezuela. Wherever I traveled, it seemed as if the genuine had been replaced by the ersatz, the essential by the luxury. In each case, the longing for something better had pushed aside the affection for something real. But when a washing machine is a luxury, it's hard to mourn (as Janice Giles couldn't) a corrugated washboard protruding from a galvanized tub.

Consequently, by the time I met Victor Thomas in West Springfield several weeks later, I took little notice of the hideous excess of strip development on Route 5, where we met for breakfast in an anonymous franchise restaurant. Blight as it was, the development was also a convenience, and no one steering into the endless parking lots had been compelled by some evil force. In fact, it was Thomas who had suggested we meet in this franchise DMZ — somehow meaningful, given that Thomas grew up in the house behind the homely, personal, deeply *authentic* market his uncle and father (14) owned in the old Merrick district of West Springfield.

14. Albert Thomas
West Springfield,
Massachusetts
(page 88)

Albert Thomas and his brother Said arrived in Massachusetts in 1914, Assyrians fleeing conscription into the Turkish army. Albert was illiterate, and Victor, his eldest child, didn't speak English until he learned it in school. There were five children in Albert's family, seven in Said's, and all the various Thomases lived together in the house behind their tiny market on Union Street.

"There are two sounds I remember from my childhood," Victor told me over coffee and eggs. "The factory whistle and the church bell." Both were the sounds of a pedestrian culture, back when people who couldn't afford cars lived where they worked, worked where they shopped, and shopped where they worshiped. The whistle came from the Gilbert & Barker plant (15), an Esso division that made gas pumps in peacetime, weaponry during World War II. G&B was across the street from the Thomas Brothers Market, and as the neighborhood people streamed to and from the factory they would stop at the market to buy what they needed. Seven days a week, from six in the morning until eleven at night, the brothers worked together in the store. When Esther Bubley took Albert's picture, he had already been behind the counter for thirty years, and he would stay there until he died, thirteen years later. Even Albert's death didn't disturb the unwrinkled curtain; his widow, Bedrea, operated the market for twenty-one years more.

15. Gilbert & Barker factory, West
Springfield, Massachusetts
(page 91)

"Don't get me wrong," Victor told me. "It was a very happy life. We had our church, we had our neighbors, we had each other." The anonymity of Route 5 was alien to Union Street, where Albert and Said extended credit to their neighbors simply because they were neighbors. Turney Moore's hired man, Paul Blake — that's Blake, holding his son Robert, in (16) — had earlier explained that he and Turney had worked shoulder to shoulder, genuine companions rather than master and laborer. "Times were tough," Blake had said, sitting at his kitchen table in Oxford, Maine, retired from

16. Paul and Robert Blake
Skowhegan, Maine
(page 132)

17. Herbert Anderson
Suffield, Connecticut
(page 163)

a career that took him from farming to dry cleaning and eventually to a supervisor's job in a sawmill. "You helped the other fellow out."

Here was a refrain that satisfied my most sentiment-hungry urges. Paul Blake's camaraderie with Turney Moore and Victor Thomas's abiding feeling for his neighbors — these instincts grow sparsely in our modern human landscape. Reginald Leslie knew that; the metal grating over the windows of his store in the North End of Hartford, the posted exhortations about Crime Watches and antidrug campaigns inside the store, were evidence too strong to ignore.

I had tracked down Leslie, a large, engaging man who looks a little like Dizzy Gillespie, only after failing to locate Herbert Anderson, a tobacco farm worker (17). Like Anderson, Leslie had been one of the several thousand West Indians who had streamed into New England during World War II to work in the Connecticut Valley tobacco fields. From 1943 onward, the Shade Growers Association, whose industry would eventually evaporate with the decline of cigar smoking, was dependent on the labor provided by a strange agreement between Great Britain and the United States. With American manpower fighting a war in Europe and the Pacific, domestic farm production was in peril. Winston Churchill, mindful of the obligations of alliance, reached into his imperial wallet and offered Franklin Roosevelt the temporary services of the crown's territorial subjects to pick up the slack.

Few in the West Indies objected; as Leslie told me, crowds of young men like himself and Herbert Anderson lined up at induction centers in the islands, desperate for a chance to come to America, however briefly, and make the kind of money that was unavailable at home. Five thousand men at a time came on the *Shank,* a U.S. naval vessel that chugged its way to New Orleans. The ship was so crowded with workers, Leslie remembered, that after receiving his daily sandwich he would return immediately to the end of the line lest he miss out on the next day's ration.

The Illinois Central took the West Indians north from New Orleans, and thousands of them reached New England via seasonal sojourns in the sugar beet fields of Michigan, the alfalfa farms of Ohio, and the Florida sugar cane plantations. Their first responsibility on arriving at the tobacco camps was to stuff straw into the mattresses they would sleep on. The Shade

Growers took a room-and-board deduction from every paycheck, and the Jamaican government set aside another, more sizable chunk as "compulsory savings." This money, held by prior arrangement in each worker's name in a Jamaican escrow account, was redeemable only back on the island, an inducement for the migrants' eventual repatriation. Farm labor didn't pay anyone particularly well, but the Jamaicans' twice-shrunk paychecks were minute.

As Leslie and I talked, we suffered a variety of interruptions — a butcher's delivery man dropping off a whole, dressed goat, groups of little children stopping by for candy. A shipment of Red Stripe beer arrived, and then a potato chip man came by to count stock. But when we began talking about the economic circumstances of the tobacco workers, I doubt Leslie could have been distracted if the building had caught fire. Leaning across the counter next to the cash register, his bright, flower-print shirt rising and falling with his extravagant gestures, his booming voice nearly pinning me to the wall, he said, "But it was okay! No one had any money, so we invented something we called a 'partner.' All of us would put our pay in a common fund. It was like a credit union. Every one of us had a number, and when your number came up you got to take four hundred dollars, for whatever you needed! Anything!"

It was a stunning notion, the spontaneous creation of a rudimentary banking system built upon communitarian bonds forged in necessity. I spoke with other veterans of the tobacco fields who confirmed that the "partners" were common practice in the camps; no one could recall anything more than the smallest disputes over their maintenance, despite the rough record-keeping, the straitened circumstances of the camps, the cultural dislocation. I asked Leslie whether he thought the same sort of institution could be created today among the people in the North End, and he dismissed the thought with a choppy wave of his hand.

For what happened to the tobacco workers after the war prefigured what would happen to people in any number of New England communities previously beset by remoteness or economic strain: entering their own version of the centrifuge, they broke the limiting bonds of isolation. Among the Jamaicans, those who won U.S. citizenship by marrying Americans began to drift away from the tobacco camps. Many went home, collected their compulsory savings money, brought it back to Hartford, and used it for down payments on homes in the North End. Still, however much one remained a member of the city's extensive West Indian community, the interdependency born of hardship dissipated. As horizons broadened, commitments narrowed. Similarly, in West Springfield, despite the sixty-four years of effort the Thomas family had put into it, Thomas Brothers became an anachronism. Neighborhood people previously constrained by their lack of mobility soon shared in the postwar prosperity and bought cars. They would still shop on credit between paydays for small items at the little market, but on the weekends they would hop in their cars and open their wallets at the supermarket. There, a feeling of freedom apparently more valuable than the sense of community that hovered around Albert Thomas's ice-cream cooler awaited them in the fluorescent aisles.

THE IMPORTANCE of the automobile in the remaking of American society can't be overestimated. It was, arguably, the most powerful agent of change the nation has ever seen. By the time Detroit had its first eight-million-car year in 1955, near-universal car ownership had obliterated urban pedestrian culture. Across the Connecticut River in Springfield, the prospect of a postwar boom had led the owners of the Springfield Public Market on Main Street (18) to expand their business. The family that had owned the store since the turn of the century decided, in 1946, to move to grander, more spacious quarters. The firm's pride was the fleet of delivery trucks that fanned out all over town each afternoon with the ingredients for a city's dinners. The market had flourished to such a degree that it would buy three hundred carloads of eggs at once.

But by the time the eight-million-automobile year arrived, if you could afford a car, you bought one; if you owned one, you used it, speeding to the supermarkets that began to ring the cities. In 1956, barely a decade after the Public Market's expansion, its doors were closed forever, the delivery trucks idle, the order-packers in their starched white coats tossed out of work.

Within a few years, most of downtown Springfield was empty, a no-man's-land of neglected buildings and empty windows. It was much the

18. Springfield Public Market
Springfield, Massachusetts
(page 96)

same in Boston and Hartford, New Haven and Providence, urban reliquaries left in the wake of suburban growth. In Framingham, west of Boston, a promoter named Houston Rawls figured that an exit from the incipient Massachusetts Turnpike most likely would be placed near the town's old sewer beds. Rawls bought up the neglected land, persuaded Jordan Marsh and Company to open a department store in his new development, then set out to convince the town fathers that what he would call Shoppers World (19) wouldn't hurt Framingham's own downtown. "Of course it hurt Framingham terribly," a man who had done publicity and promotion for Rawls told me.

19. Shoppers World
Framingham, Massachusetts
(page 78)

My informant was Frank Hatch, a former state representative and Republican gubernatorial candidate who now manages his investments from a building on Beacon Hill. When I left his office, I drove west to Shoppers World. For nearly three full miles along Route 9, an unrelieved stretch of strip development smothered the roadside. A new Ford sedan just ahead of me boasted two bumper stickers: THE SEX PISTOLS, one read; the other, I BRAKE FOR HALLUCINATIONS. Traffic squirmed forward fitfully, lanes clogged by homebound commuters. A contemporary of mine who grew up in Framingham in the 1950s had told me that today power in his hometown belonged to whomever could get permission for a curb cut on Route 9. Frank Hatch had said that Houston Rawls, a man clearly ahead of his time, had hired a powerful local lawyer, Julian Hargraves, to push his development agenda past dubious town boards. "Today," Hatch added dolefully, "you wouldn't have to." The battle was lost.

But to the commuters crawling past the flaking dome of the Jordan Marsh store at Shoppers World, much less those who did their shopping there, it was a victory — commercial development arrived in Framingham because there was a market for it. During his political career, Hatch had sponsored a successful piece of legislation that protected the state's wetlands. The measure may have retarded suburban growth in some areas, but it helped force overdevelopment in places that weren't protected. What the Framingham town boards were unwilling to do, and what Hatch's wetlands law was unable to do, was impede the basic economic urges of a mobile society. For when the countryside was opened up by the automobile and the consequent energies of the highway lobby, opportunity opened up as well. As long as you were willing to sit in traffic, you could work anywhere. When your workday was done, what was the petty aggravation of traffic compared to the piece of lawn and the comfortable house at the end of the road?

AFTER VISITING BRADFORD, VERMONT, I remembered Victor Thomas telling me that among the dozen cousins and siblings who grew up in the house on Union Street, only half stayed in West Springfield. The illiterate immigrant's son is a professor of mathematics at Holyoke Community College and a small-scale real estate entrepreneur. He still owns the building that housed the family market (it's a liquor store today) as well as the old house behind it; his mother lived there until her death, in 1987.

I thought of Thomas after my trip to Bradford because there I met thirty-three-year-old Bryce Morrill, who not only had stayed home in this Connecticut River village thirty miles southeast of Montpelier, but also continued to run the family hardware business that had been his father's and his grandfather's. Thomas had once given thought to continuing in the market business, but it didn't linger long. One of Victor's siblings settled in Alabama, another in Arkansas. His own grown children have dispersed to Florida, Washington, D.C., and upstate New York. When I asked him whether his family had scattered because of some mass Thomasian rebellion against the way of life that had held his parents in one building for more than six decades, he said, "My family has gone its own way for the same reason that all families do. The forces of economics are stronger than the forces of kinship."

For most of the people I met, Thomas's statement contained the incontrovertible truth of aphorism, but for Bryce Morrill it didn't hold. He had gone off to college in Boston, studying to be an architectural draftsman, but he soon returned to Bradford and took over the family store.

Bart Morrill, Bryce's father, is the broad-shouldered man in (20), and by all accounts this convivial moment shared in conversation with one of his customers was characteristic. Twelve years after his death, most people in Bradford still call the Gove & Morrill hardware store "Bart's." His son told me that as a boy he would often overhear customers talking about what

20. Bart Morrill and customer
Bradford, Vermont
(page 126)

a wonderful man his father was. "He loved his work," Bryce said, "and everyone knew it."

Gove & Morrill has moved next door to the building in the picture, but upstairs in Bryce's office it didn't take me long to discern the presence of Bart's time. On one side of the long, narrow room, an exquisite built-in pine cabinet stretched to the ceiling. On the walls hung prewar advertising signs that a fern-bar manager would sacrifice a week's receipts to own — LICENSED TO SELL POWDER, read one. Bryce, a compact, friendly man in flannel and corduroy, sat at a rolltop desk, its top shelf supporting an array of antique gadgets. Only the phone, the sort of European-style model one might find in a modern art museum, betrayed the intrusion of the present.

When Bryce came back from Boston, he told me, he wasn't certain that he wanted to stay in the hardware business, but he knew that city life made him uncomfortable. "Then," he told me, "one night in nineteen seventy-five, a fire broke out, and I walked downtown at three in the morning to see what had happened. I remember telling myself that if the store was still standing, then that was where I'd be."

Bart died suddenly the next year, and Bryce took over. He was twenty-two. "I've never regretted being here," he said. "But it's different from my father's time. Back in the forties, this was the only game in town. Now there's an Aubuchon store six doors away, a Western Auto outlet on Main Street. South of town there's a lumber and home center, a farm store, and two more lumberyards. Fourteen miles north, there's another lumberyard and a hardware store."

But competition didn't bother him, Bryce said; competition was inevitable. "We're not price conscious," he continued. "We specialize in service. What I like is when someone comes in with a broken faucet and wants to buy a new one, and I can see it can be fixed with a one-dollar part. So I'll spend half an hour down in the shop for the one-dollar sale." The postmodern phone rang discreetly, and Bryce spoke for a few moments with his mother, who still lives in Bradford. The brief interruption apparently changed his mood, or at least let reality seep upstairs from the store into his burnished sanctum. An odd look, at once sorrowful and a little angry, settled on his face when we resumed our conversation. "People used to know this as the place that had the item you couldn't find anywhere else, but the companies that supplied that sort of thing are out of business," he said, his words accelerating, his pitch rising. "Our stock is pretty run-of-the-mill now. You go to a shelf to find an item that used to be hand-made, and now it's in a blister pack on the wall. To succeed in this business you've got to do things like direct mail, you've got to use hyped-up marketing for an inferior product, and I don't like it."

His explosion over, Bryce exhaled, settled down. "I guess my kids won't be at this desk in thirty years," he said. His tone didn't reflect disappointment so much as an acknowledgment that his stand against the present was some kind of personal eccentricity, an inexplicable foible.

I had arranged with Bryce to meet his mother after we were through, and as we walked down the aisle of his showroom to the door, two salesmen brought him up to date on small matters of business; he responded with the same good-natured charm he had displayed when we had first met, and then he opened the door for me. As he gave me directions to his mother's house, he was standing virtually in the same position Bart occupied in the photograph. Two passersby said hello; he waved back. The exasperation over the blister packs and the inferior goods seemed days past. By all appearances, he was a contented man, aware of the anachronistic life he had chosen but satisfied that he had made the right choice, as he was sure his father had.

After I left Bryce, I drove to his mother's neat, pale yellow house overlooking the town and the plain beyond. A small, quiet woman in her sixties, she agreed — with a certain wariness — to talk with me about her husband. She brought out some large scrapbooks, and after pausing over various pieces of homely, small-town news, we came to the page that commemorated the fire that had inspired Bryce's decision to stay in the hardware business. Then she paused to relate something the clippings didn't tell: not long before Bart died, he had put the store up for sale. Business was bad, the competition was growing daily, and he had had enough of it.

But then Bart died, and Bryce took over a way of life that itself had died years before. When I asked his mother what she thought her husband would have done without the business that had sustained him emotionally for so long, she said, "I doubt that he knew."

THE SAD THING in this country today," Ray McLaughlin had told me, speaking of farming, "is that young people who want to do something the old way don't have the chance." Turney Moore's brother-in-law had never been a farmer himself, but he came from a farm family that lived in a handsome house on the banks of the Kennebec. We were gazing at the old McLaughlin place from Ray's new house, a passive-solar retirement home he had built from a plan he had purchased for $2 after reading about it in *The Christian Science Monitor.* In the valley below us, the old house looked as if it had been washed and combed for an appearance in *Architectural Digest.* It is now owned by a wealthy family from Waterville, Maine; a riding ring was the acreage's most prominent feature.

As we stood on his porch, I asked McLaughlin whether it was difficult to look each day at the home he had lived in for seventy-three years. "I don't look at it that way," he said. "What I see is a house too hard to take care of." A similar sentiment, I imagine, had provoked Bart Morrill's decision to give up the hardware store just before the heart attack that killed him at fifty-five. But Bryce Morrill, despite the second-rate parts hanging on his store's walls, was insulated from that sort of despair. What protected him was the most durable sort of nostalgia — the nostalgia for something that never really existed.

It's no surprise that the past looks prettiest to those who haven't lived through it. The screech of television that I abhor, the blister packs that offend Bryce Morrill, the march of the malls and the curb cuts that repel my friend from Framingham — none of us has ever really known a world without them. But our imaginings are far prettier than the more accurate memories of people a generation older. To them, looking back, radio was naïve, one-of-a-kind hardware items impractical and inconvenient, the corner market overpriced and understocked. Memory may be selective, but imagined memory is as narrow as a tunnel.

But there's something else, too, that falsely sweetens the past for the postwar generation. What we have that our parents generally did not is a matched set of luxuries. The first is choice, the freedom to escape from the preordained. Turney Moore's succession to his father's domain was inescapable; John Moore's flight to college, graduate school, and an

21. Horse carriages
Lyndonville, Vermont
(page 157)

22. Marion Brown
Somerville, Maine
(page 82)

engineering career was propelled by the social explosion ignited at the war's end, and the atomized mist of a hundred choices that settled on the newly booming society.

The second luxury is taste, the by-product of choice. Presented with achievable options, we are free to select the most appealing one. Browsing through life's store, we look for what intrigues or amuses or charms. The young, well-off family that bought Ray McLaughlin's house could appreciate its classical lines and the handsome fields that surrounded it. But even now, McLaughlin couldn't see beyond the burden of responsibility that the house had always represented. Contemporary eyes can look at the roughhewn carriage in (21) covetously; to its owner, it was something to be discarded as soon as he could afford a car.

In some ways, what obliterated Ryan Drug, the neighborhood pharmacy in Springfield, Massachusetts (7), was the first expression of postwar taste, brought on by the prospering society's sudden discovery of choices that hadn't existed a decade earlier. The picture doesn't show what was inside Ryan's: a marble and mahogany soda fountain stretching along one wall, a pressed-tin ceiling hovering over the glass-and-wood library cases that sheltered the drugstore's stock. When I visited Springfield's North End, Donald Ryan, whose grandfather started, in 1895, what is now a chain of five stores, presided at the branch that succeeded the one in the picture, just up Main Street from the original. "I remember when we tore out the soda fountain, replaced the library cases with open gondolas, and put in a dropped acoustical ceiling," Ryan told me. "In the early fifties, those things were old-fashioned, and there was nothing worse than being old-fashioned." He smiled. "Boy, what you'd have to pay for those today!"

Back then, they could have been had for their scrap value. The forties occupied the last moment when what we now value as antique or charming still surrounded us. Marion Brown, of Somerville, Maine (22), isn't cleaning all those shapely kerosene lamps because she plans to put them on display or sell them to a dealer. She's cleaning them because, in 1944, Somerville didn't have electricity. After the war, when the nation's newly stoked engines brought power to the darkest corners of New England, the same lamps became symbols of a meanness their owners hoped quickly to forget. Physical manifestations of the past became objects of derision and neglect.

Even more than the soda fountain and the tin ceiling, what really affronted the taste of the 1950s was the neighborhood that Ryan Drug served. The North End had long been Springfield's immigrant quarter, and by World War II it had become a largely black enclave. It was a thickly populated neighborhood, "full of life," Ryan recalled, but, by the perceptions of the time, hopelessly ill-suited for the era's imagined ideal of life. The sensibility that could see no value in a marble soda fountain was likely to be blind to anything that wasn't modern. "Plastic" had not yet become an epithet. Boxy rectangles of brick and glass were admired for their sleekness, their newness.

When the nation looked at its inner-city neighborhoods, it was sensibility as much as sympathy that brought in the bulldozers. "Urban renewal" meant urban destruction, the obliteration of a physical stain. It made the downtown of a city like Worcester, Massachusetts, look like a Dresden rebuilt after saturation bombing. Americans were so obsessed with newness that, according to the federal criteria that determined whether housing was substandard, residential buildings of a certain age were *by legal definition* suspect — it wasn't their condition that doomed them so much as their age. Neighborhoods such as Springfield's North End, where the vast majority of homes were turn-of-the-century antiques, got the death sentence. Springfield still calls itself The City of Homes, but by the mid-1960s it had used vast quantities of state and federal funds to destroy 1,300 of them, along with 355 business establishments, including Ryan Drug.

A step behind the bulldozers came the construction teams. The 105-acre renewal site in the North End saw low-rise, low-density government offices and private businesses sprout from the rubble that once had been street after street of aged houses. One such home, on Tenth Street, had belonged to the mother of David Rankin, the newsboy in (23). A WPA photograph of the Rankin house on file in the Springfield building department reveals a simple, well maintained, two-story wooden home with a picket fence in front. Then renewal came and wiped out the house — wiped out Tenth Street itself. Rankin, who lived with his mother, had sold his papers at the corner of Main and Bridge streets for nearly two decades. When I visited downtown Springfield, I met Pete Slepchuk, who

23. David Rankin
Springfield, Massachusetts
(page 95)

has owned a pinball arcade–turned–video game parlor for forty-three years on Main Street, one block from where David Rankin sold his papers. Slepchuk remembered Rankin as a sweet-natured, slightly dull-witted soul who likely wouldn't have been able to cope with the wrench of forced change. "I guess he just died," Slepchuk told me.

Later, I learned that David Rankin's end was less tidy than that. His mother having died just a few years before a wrecker's ball came to Tenth Street, Rankin was cut adrift when the demolition began. Unable to look after himself, he was committed to the state hospital in Northampton, where he lived among the insane for the rest of his life.

One could argue that David Rankin was lucky; in Northampton, at least, he was cared for. Had he been less simple, he probably would have found his way to one of the five towers of the publicly assisted Riverview Apartments, along with the other North Enders who didn't know better than to live in older homes that didn't meet the era's standards of taste. There, Rankin would have found no bus service to get him to his downtown corner, no grocery in which to shop. The neighborhood stores didn't reopen at Riverview; the hardier ones, like Ryan Drug, moved into new quarters, and the rest simply vanished. The section of the North End in which Rankin had lived belongs to IBM, to faceless medical offices, and to the new plant of Springfield Newspapers, the company that made the papers he sold.

The newspaper company, as it happened, put up its dull loaf of a building on precisely the spot where Ryan Drug had once stood. Don Ryan relocated the store to another treeless block on Main Street. You know the place — there's one like it everywhere. An asphalt parking lot fronts the drugstore and the other establishments in its ugly little mall. Inside the drugstore, fluorescent lights and electronic antitheft devices gaze upon anonymous rows of packaged products.

B	UT I SAW ANOTHER expression of modern America emblazoned in Ryan's window. A sign proclaimed that the prescription department accepts Medex 3, Medicaid, Master Health Plus, Health New England, Healthy Start — a roster, in all, of twelve reimbursement plans that didn't exist when David Rankin left the corner of Main and Bridge for the wards of the state hospital. The sense of possibility that had opened up in the postwar years manifested itself first in the "improvement" that started the bulldozers roaming through the North End; by the early 1970s, that same instinct had penetrated the social bedrock so thoroughly that once-powerless groups could claim powers and rights unimagined just a generation earlier.

When the North End demolition was first proposed, public hearings in Springfield's Municipal Auditorium brought forth the testimony of 106 speakers, only two of whom spoke against the program. The postwar belief in newness had ignited the notion of urban renewal, and it was fueled by an abiding willingness to concede to government and to the business community the shaping prerogatives of our culture. If major institutions were not all-knowing, they were still all-powerful. There isn't a city in America that doesn't bear the telltale marks of the government and business omnipotence of the 1950s: the deadened tombstones of newer-is-better architecture, the clogged arteries of a transportation idea that supplanted public transit. Then, almost overnight, a critical part of the social contract was ripped up and redrafted. As it turned out, the two lonely dissidents at the Municipal Auditorium were heralds of a great cultural shift. Soon twin impulses arose that would have made the destruction of the North End impossible: empowerment and entitlement.

One afternoon during my travels, I visited with George Keverian, the speaker of the Massachusetts House of Representatives, in his ornate, high-ceilinged office at the State House on Beacon Hill in Boston. Keverian represents Everett, the mostly ethnic, blue-collar enclave where he grew up. When we met, he was engaged in a legislative battle surrounding an effort to choose a site for an industrial concern deemed essential to greater Boston. Keverian and his allies wanted to shove the facility, a car-crushing plant, into one of the wealthy bedroom communities west of the city. Everett and its dingy industrial neighbors, once boastful of their smokestacks, had had enough.

But when Gordon Parks arrived in town in 1944, Everett liked its refineries, its chemical concerns, its electrical generating plants, and likely would have considered the car-crushing facility as another badge on its laboring chest. "We used to talk about industry in Everett with some pride," Keverian said. Esso had been one of the city's industrial mainstays, its

24. Pete McCauley
Everett, Massachusetts
(page 121)

25. Connecticut River
South Deerfield, Massachusetts
(page 124)

refinery along the Mystic River employing five hundred people, including the welder in (24). Today, all that remains of the company's muscular presence is a distribution terminal and a white-collar staff ensconced in a bland, comfortable, two-story office building.

The refinery didn't close because the people of Everett rose up against it. In fact, I saw on the office wall of one former Esso employee a photograph of the parties who helped to keep the refinery open when the company first wanted to shut it down: a young Senator Edward Kennedy and a brush-cut Charles Colson, who was at the time an aide to Senator Leverett Saltonstall (several years before Colson began executing dirty tricks for Richard Nixon). Kennedy had threatened an attack on the then-sacred oil depletion allowance if Esso pulled out, and Saltonstall went along for the ride. In time, though, even political muscle couldn't have persuaded the people of Everett to replace it with another, comparable industrial concern.

The change that George Keverian saw in his hometown was at work in a thousand other communities as well. "The world is different today," he told me. "If you locate a liquor store in a residential neighborhood, five hundred people will turn out to protest it. Back then" — back in the 1940s — "people were too busy making a living. And they trusted government to make the right decisions."

Keverian is a huge man, and the heave of his shoulders when he said this nearly caused his office chandelier to shudder. His exasperation stood well for scores of other politicians who have seen the authority of their species eroded by litigation, deregulation, competing interests — but mostly by a citizenry that can, for the right issue, get as aroused as the Revolutionary patriots who are buried just a block away from Keverian's office. Today, one couldn't imagine a government agency bespoiling the lush Connecticut River Valley farmlands (25) by slicing them in half with the construction of I-91, as had happened in the late 1950s. The doomed nuclear power plant that stands idle in Seabrook, New Hampshire, could have been built and activated without complaint thirty years ago.

When I left Keverian's office, I thought about an image that had been in my mind when I met Victor Thomas in West Springfield: contented workers, lunch boxes in hand, as they streamed across Union Street into the Gilbert & Barker factory — workers like the war-mustered women lining up at the G & B time clock (26). I had been chasing the Esso pictures long enough to know that the image was a mirage of sorts, that the wages of hardship and the strain of struggle up the social ladder exhausted many of these workers and stripped them to varying degrees of rawness. But Keverian had made me see another presence that lingered in these lives — the grey, hovering hand of powerlessness.

No, it was even more severe than that — it was the belief so many Americans once had that, unless born to power, they had no right to its privileges. In New England, the dividing wall that kept wealthy, rooted Yankees in control and closed the avenues of power to immigrants and their children hadn't yet fractured. The fumes that the Everett refinery emitted in 1944 were no less noxious to the city's working population than those that, a generation later, would provoke clean air legislation, federal enforcement codes, and the occupation of the workplace by health and safety inspectors. What would in time become more potent were the demands of a society that felt newly entitled.

What, I wondered, would an empowered David Rankin have asked for? The right to stay in his home on Tenth Street? Free prescription drugs? Both of these things, and likely many more. For people in circumstances such as his, these things had become the boats in the barn. For them, the luxury to choose had mutated into the luxury to demand.

APART FROM THE SMALL Berkshire town in which I live (where at least an architectural version of the precious past hides the microwaves in the kitchens and the garden tractors in the garages), I have long considered Gloucester, Massachusetts, my favorite New England place. It's only a fifty-minute drive from Boston, yet it feels in no way suburban. The harbor boasts far more working boats than leisure craft. New immigrants, mostly Italian and Portuguese, have helped the place retain its rich ethnic feeling, and you can eat better here for less money than anywhere else in New England. As in other small cities throughout the region, the malls that sucked the chain stores away from downtown several years ago have left Main Street to locally owned businesses — pictures (27) and (28) show who owned the downtowns of the 1940s: chain stores and franchises as ubiquitous as they would become

26. Gilbert & Barker factory West Springfield, Massachusetts
(page 90)

27. Metropolitan Chain Store Norwich, Connecticut
(page 53)

28. Neisner's Springfield, Massachusetts
(page 94)

at the malls. In Gloucester today, history's remnants aren't props on a stage set. Gloucester is a veritable temple of authenticity.

For centuries, it has been a fishing port. The smells of sea and fish are everywhere on the waterfront, from the hall of the Seafarers International Union to the huge Gorton processing plant. When it isn't the sea one smells, it's the scent of deep-fry batter from one of the seafood restaurants that seem to be everywhere. I wandered into the SIU hall one morning to find a large, linoleum-floored room, empty except for a few older men playing cribbage at a table near one of the oceanside windows. If they had looked out, they would have seen rehabilitated buildings nearby, and a stylish restaurant where the Bloody Marys bear huge stalks of celery as if they are flags signaling the onset of gentrification. But Sam Loiachino and the other retired fishermen I spoke with didn't look out. They could only look back.

It required no leap at all for Loiachino and his companions to return to the days when the Esso photographer was in town. As I began riffling through the stack of pictures I had brought with me, I was stopped immediately. "That's the *Riggs*," one of the men said, placing his beefy, roughened finger on an image he had seen for less than a second (29). The *Eliza C. Riggs,* a sixty-ton craft of the type called a gill-netter, wasn't an especially impressive vessel, but these men had a memory for fishing boats the way a ballplayer has a memory for the pitchers he has faced.

The *Riggs* belonged to the Franco-Indian LaFond family, who came to Gloucester from the Great Lakes in the early part of the century. John R. Lafond — the family was divided in its devotion to the capital *F* — had visited the area and learned, simply enough, that there were more fish in the ocean than in the lakes. With his son Bill (30), John bought the *Riggs* around 1920, and Bill continued to run the boat from his own wharf, with his sons, Randy and Ellsworth, until well into the 1940s. While roaming through some old books in the Gloucester library, I discovered that the postmodernist poet Charles Olson had spent a teenage summer gill-netting aboard the *Riggs*. In his *Maximus* poems, Olson wrote about one of the crewmen: "Jake, his name/was, mate aboard the Lafonds'/gill-netters./When I knew him his nails/were all gone, peeled away from the brine they'd been in all the days of/his life."

A contemporary wanderer on the Gloucester waterfront today can

29. *Eliza C. Riggs*
Gloucester, Massachusetts
(page 69)

30. Bill LaFond
(with pipe), Gloucester,
Massachusetts
(page 68)

find hands like that everywhere. The size of the fleet, though, is a fraction of what it once was. Between 1967 and 1972 alone, the number of working boats in Gloucester had shrunk by nearly half. Stanley Wang, an economist with the National Marine Fisheries Service, showed me reams of statistics that established the economic impossibility of the industry: as demand for fish has increased in our health-conscious culture, prices have risen; as prices rise, the waters get fished out. Even farmers have it better, controlling their land's production by planting one crop this year, another one next year. But on the ocean, where there are no property lines, the fisherman who wishes to let the biological stock replenish itself will be trumped by the competitor who wants to cash his check today. In 1963, the average tow for haddock in the waters worked by Gloucestermen yielded ninety-nine pounds of fish; by 1986, the same tow pulled in only eight pounds.

In Gloucester's glistening old city hall, a WPA mural in the city council chamber bears the motto, "Build not for today but for tomorrow as well." The sentiment mocks the lives of the city's fishermen. Upstairs, Gloucester fisheries commissioner Tony Verga told me how prankish kids used to run from the police while jumping from boat to boat, a full mile along the waterfront. Even then, Verga said, when Gloucester produced more of the nation's food fish than any other port, "people were saying that the industry didn't make sense any more. And they're still saying it today." But I had seen so much activity around the huge Gorton plant on Rogers Street. Surely an operation like that wouldn't be reinvesting in a hopeless cause? "Gorton's hasn't bought a pound of fish off a Gloucester boat in years," Verga said. "They're processing huge frozen blocks of fish shipped in from Sweden." One of Stanley Wang's colleagues had earlier asked me if I had seen "all those forty-year-old boats on the waterfront." Of course I had; the display of ships on the waterfront, even if not so grand as it had been in Tony Verga's boyhood, was one of the sights that made Gloucester such an arresting place. "They're there," the government man said, "only because they don't have any debt, they don't have any insurance, and they don't have any future."

All of this hadn't changed in decades either. Then and now, men worked the boats until they were seized in bankruptcy, dynamited, or simply allowed to fall apart. The *Riggs* limped along until Randy Lafond let it sink in the late forties. But to the end, the old boat made its daily voyages to where the pollack waited, bringing in seven thousand pounds one day, four thousand the next. Morning after morning, well before dawn, Randy or his brother would arrive at the waterfront, find Ed Townsend (31, center) passed out on the wharf from a night of drinking, toss his body on deck, and hope that he would come to before they reached the fishing waters. Edgar Decker, the engineer standing in front of Townsend, was a more solid type. He once tried to make a life on shore as a barber, but he soon found himself called back to sea. Offered a chance to engineer on a tug in New York Harbor, Decker needed to put in two voyages on hundred-ton vessels to qualify. On the second one, a fog set in, and the captain asked Decker to go belowdecks to cut the engines so they might hear any approaching boats. While the engineer was in the hold, a vessel rammed the ship in the side, and Decker drowned.

All over Gloucester I heard stories like these. It seemed as if everyone here, except for the occupants of the great shingle cottages on the Back Shore and the stone palaces of Eastern Point, fished at one time or another, or was related to someone who did. And for every picture I had, someone could give me a tale of sorrow. A boy whose picture was on his tombstone — killed by lightning while standing on a wharf. The man memorialized with his daughter (32) — he pulled up his net to find a shark in it, killed the intruder with a shotgun kept on board for just such an event, then took a blast in his own midsection when the boat lurched. Joseph Frontiera bled to death in his brother's arms, somewhere off Point Judith.

One night I was dining with a friend in a Portuguese restaurant on the Gloucester waterfront, attacking a plate of quail in green sauce. It was late, and a few beers, as well as the unnoticed departure of the other customers and the din they had brought to the place, had me talking louder than usual. I was also fueled by my astonishment at the tragedy that seemed to hover over this sad, inbred community; by now, the loveliness of its damnable authenticity seemed infinitely paler. I showed my guest a picture of one man I hadn't been able to locate, a fellow the men at the union hall had identified as "Nigger Joe" Pallazola (33). I told her that I'd talked to half a dozen people named Pallazola, but this Pallazola was apparently from a different family. It was then that the waitress interrupted my near shouting and asked if she

31. Ed Townsend (center), Edgar Decker (front), Gloucester, Massachusetts
(page 66)

32. Frontiera family tombstone Gloucester, Massachusetts
(page 72)

could look at the picture. "That's my father-in-law," she said.

Her name was Margie Pallazola, and she told me that Joe was dead. After he decided to retire in the late 1960s, he towed the *Rosie and Grace*, his 110-foot converted World War I submarine chaser, out past Marblehead, dynamited it, and watched it sink. "After that," Margie said, "Joe seemed to lose his will to live."

The restaurant had been closed, the register receipts counted, and the tables cleaned for the morning. Margie Pallazola sat down with my friend and me, and talked at length about the fishing industry, her father-in-law, life in Gloucester. After a while, I asked whether her husband was a fisherman. "Well, Jerry *was* a fisherman," she said, "for thirty-five years, until he stopped and we opened a restaurant." She was telling us this with the matter-of-factness she had earlier used to explain the menu. "But one day in nineteen seventy-eight," she went on, "a cousin of his was shorthanded, so Jerry went out to the Grand Banks to help him. Then he did it again a few times." On his fourth trip, the *Captain Cosmo* never came back.

The next morning, I went back to the city hall to see if I could find Jerry Pallazola's name on the third-floor mural that lists the names of all those lost at sea in Gloucester. It wasn't that I doubted his widow; I think I simply wanted to register my own small act of mourning in a community that seemed to mourn more than any one place should have to. The names are arranged chronologically, and in some years in the distant past there are twenty or thirty people memorialized. Coming down to the present era, as the industry itself has shrunk, so has the honor roll of the dead. Some years bear no names at all. But 1978 is full with the names of Jerry Pallazola and his shipmates. Later, back in the library, I read about the nine-day air-and-sea search that had covered 121,000 square miles of the North Atlantic and uncovered no trace of the *Captain Cosmo*. The *Gloucester Daily Times*'s chronicle of the search revealed the citywide sharing of the families' grief as well. Special masses were held at churches that had witnessed such rituals many times before. But, as one Gloucesterite said, "It's like the sea just swallowed them up."

Just before my friend and I had left the restaurant the night before, Margie Pallazola had said, "Sometimes I still think Jerry will be coming back, walking up the hill."

33. "Nigger Joe" Pallazola
Gloucester, Massachusetts
(page 70)

34. Ellsworth Lafond
Gloucester, Massachusetts
(page 71)

ON MY LAST DAY IN GLOUCESTER, I found Bill LaFond's surviving son, Randy, working on an old wooden boat tied up to a sagging wharf, next door to the wharf Bill had once owned, where the restaurant with the declarative Bloody Marys now stands. Randy was eighty when we met, a stocky, pink-faced man whose bright eyes widened with each story he told. He remembered the poet Olson. He told me how his brother Ellsworth (34) had given up fishing in his late fifties, taken a job on land, and dropped dead of a heart attack. He explained how his father's muddled estate led him to abandon the *Riggs* and let it rot: he was doing all the work, but the boat's share of the proceeds had to be divided with relatives who didn't work, and it just wasn't worth it to him any longer. Randy had stories the way the wharf itself had barnacles, an inexhaustible supply of stories. It was as if Gloucester's fund of recollection was directly proportional to its share of pain.

Randy worked on his boat while we talked, scuttling about on deck like some amphibious creature building a home in a dune. "I retired in nineteen sixty-five," Randy told me. "But five years ago, I bought the *Liberty* and put in my own engine. I'm a gentleman fisherman. I go out almost every day, just me and my wife. I don't take anyone else 'cause I don't want to pay for the insurance. I've been going sixty-two years now," he continued. "It's all I've ever done."

A bright sun was rising in the sky, and now and again another fisherman would stop by to chat. Randy knew everybody on the waterfront. An older, Portuguese man named Manuel stopped by for a while, and Randy told me after he'd left that they always helped each other out. From the wharfside I could see into the union hall, the old men still at their cribbage. As Randy Lafond and I passed the time, the sad songs of Gloucester slowly took on a different harmony. Through every tragedy and every hardship, someone had been helping out someone else, or making it possible for yet another to survive his grief. Personal weaknesses like Ed Townsend's were forgiven because there was work to be done; neighborly loyalties like the one Jerry Pallazola felt for his shorthanded cousin were celebrated in the community's heart.

Gloucester was a hopelessly outmoded place, the only one I had visited that actually had slipped backward on the economic scale since the 1940s.

In the fishing community, ambition was absent, and other possibilities alien. Randy Lafond's son, Bill, fished, and Bill's teenaged son, John Randolph, intended to fish as well — a fifth generation pulling the nets, riding the water, defying the potency of nature and the fickleness of the market. It made no sense, this business, nor did this way of life. In Gloucester, where authenticity — by now, for me, a severely tarnished prize — was everywhere, logic had surrendered to sentiment.

But this same sentiment had preserved something that coexisted with the limited, powerless, and essentially constricting life of the 1940s that so many people had recalled for me. In the Gloucester of the late 1980s — as in Skowhegan or West Springfield or the Connecticut Valley tobacco camps of the forties — I had found an unshakable feeling of community. Once we were involved in our neighbors' lives. Then the luscious prospect of freedom, opportunity, empowerment, and material comfort made us less dependent on one another. We turned toward the boats in the barn and away from the neighbor up the road. "This is the age of the individual, not the family," Victor Thomas had told me. When our progress presented its bill, the loss of community was the most expensive entry on the ledger.

BUT CAN WE really put a price on any of it? How can we say that the choices most New Englanders, and most Americans, have made were the wrong ones? In Windsor, Connecticut, where I had visited the long, low, concrete-block barracks of one of the last of the tobacco camps, the dusty fields were ringed by new subdivisions called Fox Hollow, Strawberry Hills, and Woodfield Crossing, each obliterating the natural features it had been named for. One couldn't possibly imagine a "partner," like the one Reginald Leslie had described, emerging among the serene suburban acres of Strawberry Hills, but it would be preposterous to suggest the coarse reality of the tobacco camps was more virtuous than the anonymous comfort of the subdivisions. Who could ask John Moore, comfortable in Oregon, to trade his life for the strain of farm life that had defeated his father in Maine? Victor Thomas could have kept his family's market alive — but why should he have? Gloucester has its feeling of community, but largely because it has very little else.

Inescapably, we long for what's irretrievable and simultaneously

35. Jewelry factory
Pawtucket, Rhode Island
(page 173)

36. General store, Albion, Maine
(page 158)

undervalue what surrounds us. In 1937, John Cheever looked about him and wrote of New England, "The glorious seaboard of the China trade [now] means to most of us . . . empty harbors and fugitive mill towns and the smell of the tourist camps and a cretin at a gas station." Was his fugitive mill town populated with the stately industrial buildings like those in Todd Webb's picture of Pawtucket, Rhode Island, which look so appealing in the photograph (35)? Was Cheever's idea of the "cretin at the gas station" one of the men on the porch of Libby Bros., in Albion, Maine (36), men who look only noble to modern eyes? Cheever was a young man when he wrote those words, like Bryce Morrill, aching for something as imaginary as it was distant. Forty years from now, will someone travel around New England and lament the demolition of the shopping malls, the extinction of satellite dishes?

I made one last stop on my journeys on a June Tuesday. Heading to New York on business, I detoured to the lower Connecticut River town of Chester. One of the prettiest villages in all New England, it is a sparklingly preserved collection of Colonial houses owned by commuters to Hartford and New Haven, weekenders from New York, and smart pensioners who knew to hold on to the family property back when Chester was just another forgotten town in a forgotten valley. On a previous trip, I recalled, I had seen a sign directing the traveler to the Chester–Hadlyme Ferry — the ferry in picture (37).

I went looking for it, and soon the ferry slip on the river's west bank appeared ahead of me. As I waited in line with two other cars, I could clearly see the boat departing the slip on the Hadlyme side. It turned out to be the *Selden III,* which had replaced the picture's *Selden II* not long after Charlotte Brooks had brought her camera to Chester in 1946. It had a two-story wheelhouse, but otherwise nothing was different except the vintage of the cars on board. Of all the Esso pictures, this was the one that revealed the least change.

After a few minutes' wait, I drove aboard the *Selden III,* handed my seventy-five cents to an elderly man in a pressed khaki uniform, and set out for Hadlyme. Two workmen in a pickup occupied the deck space to my right. A big Buick driven by a woman in wraparound sunglasses was wedged in behind us.

How strange it was. Just five miles to the north, at East Haddam, a broad bridge crossed the river. If there was a need for this ferry, it escaped me. It seemed as if I had stumbled into some pocket of New England where history's centrifuge had broken down, where the men in the pickup and the woman in the Buick and the amiable crewmen hadn't been hurtled outward into some delicious prospect of the future.

Only later, when my travels were finally over, did I learn why the Chester–Hadlyme Ferry still runs, why this one photograph from four decades ago had not been turned by time into an archival representation of a distant world. It is owned by the state of Connecticut, which subsidizes losses amounting to $100,000 a year. Local legislators keep the ferry alive because they feel it is a valuable piece of our heritage. It isn't a survivor from the past at all; it's a museum.

But what's wrong with that? The impulse to preserve and remember the past, after all, is New England's genius. It's only when we want to relive the past, to want not only to hold it in our hearts, but also to have it once again in our hands, that we dishonor what it means.

Almost a year after I visited Bradford, Vermont, word came that Bryce Morrill had put the family hardware store up for sale. Even he, the most steadfast nostalgist I'd met, had decided to let go of the ungraspable ghosts.

37. Chester–Hadlyme Ferry
Chester, Connecticut
(page 86)

The Photographs

Donat Premont, of Northfield, Vermont, the son of woolen mill workers, was eight when the Esso photographer visited the South Village Superior School and captured his efforts at reading. Seven years later, having completed the eighth grade, Premont left school permanently.

The South Village school was one of four one-room schoolhouses in Northfield; all were closed in 1978.

The Pleasantdale section of South Portland, Maine, where the Lobstertorium once stood, remains one of the few neighborhoods in that once-industrial city that hasn't been claimed by suburbanization and rapidly escalating real estate prices.

This roadside landmark on Route 6, in Onset, Massachusetts, on Cape Cod, was demolished in the 1950s. Its owner, the Ocean Spray canning cooperative, has seen its cranberry production increase threefold since the photograph was taken in 1947.

American Woolen's Wood Mill, in Lawrence, Massachusetts, was once the largest textile plant in the world, harboring 7,000 employees. After the New England textile industry collapsed, the immense factory, one third of a mile long, was left empty. It was later resuscitated in the high-tech boom by Honeywell-Bull, which today employs 800 people manufacturing computer systems in its 1,200,000 square feet.

For thirty-eight years, the Boston Braves played their home schedule at Braves Field on the south bank of the Charles River. After New England's only National League baseball team departed for Milwaukee in 1953, Boston University purchased the stadium. Since then, it has been used as a university sports complex, although various portions have been demolished to make room for the Massachusetts Turnpike and for BU dormitories.

In 1945, St. Jerome's was one of three Catholic high schools in the industrial city of Holyoke, Massachusetts, and Father Timothy Leary (front) was both director of the school and of athletics. Only one parochial high school remains in Holyoke today, and Father Leary — now a monsignor — presides over cemeteries for the Springfield diocese.

Aroostook County, Maine

The northernmost tip of Maine boomed in 1894, when the completion of the Bangor & Aroostook railway brought it suddenly within reach of the markets for its dominant export: potatoes. When photographer Gordon Parks visited in 1947, the county was riding a boom like none it had ever seen. The federal government had begun subsidizing potato farmers earlier in the decade and found itself paying the growers to dump their crops after the war. The county was planted fencerow to fencerow, Canadian workers flooded into the area at harvest time, and virtually everyone in the area prospered.

Then, in 1951, subsidies ended. But Aroostook remained tied umbilically to the potato, with a one-crop economy dependent upon the success of a commodity better suited to the weather and topography of Idaho and other western states. An unwillingness, or perhaps inability, to diversify crops have led to a sharp decline in Aroostook's prosperity, and by 1987 more than three quarters of the county's farmers were in debt, some as much as $3,000 an acre.

A worker on the Charles Hussey farm in Presque Isle. In 1947, a good picker could earn, in 1989 dollars, as much as $150 a day plus room and board; the same picker today earns barely one third of that.

Harvest on the Hussey farm. The Aroostook schools still close for the annual harvest, a ritual dating back to the turn of the century.

Potato-dusting helicopter. Developed by the Kaman Corporation, of Bloomfield, Connecticut, it proved to be less than efficient: the whirling blades churned spray into pilots' eyes, which in turn led to repeated crashes.

French Canadian workers, Fred Lausier Farm, Presque Isle. As many as 5,000 Canadians used to cross the border for the harvest season each fall, first posting bonds to ensure their return when the harvest was over.

Potato farmer with hayrake, Presque Isle. In the late 1940s, Aroostook County farmers had nearly 200,000 acres in potatoes. Today, western competition has reduced that number by more than half.

During the 1940s, Mark Kramer, who owned the Harvard Book Store, in Cambridge, Massachusetts, sold $20,000 worth of used textbooks per year out of 800 square feet of space in Harvard Square. His son Frank, who took over in 1962, abandoned textbooks for general titles and opened a cafe on the premises. He has seen his space expand to 6,500 square feet and brought the store's annual volume to $2,000,000.

The oldest university in America, in 1949, revolved around a Harvard Yard that today remains, physically, much as it was forty years before. What has changed is the complexion of the faces that occupy it: by the late 1980s nonwhite enrollment had reached nearly sixteen percent of the student body.

These routemen for the Hood Milk Company, in western Massachusetts, would see their jobs disappear by the early 1960s. What had once been a near-universal system of home milk delivery succumbed to the spread of convenience stores, improved refrigeration technology, and high labor costs.

In Marblehead, Massachusetts, suburbanization transformed the old seafaring town. The Hotel Leslie (at right) was razed to make way for waterfront townhouses; the Hotel Glover (at center) was relocated and converted into expensive apartments.

Before regional malls pulled them into the suburbs, national chains and franchise operations dominated most of New England's downtowns, such as this one, in Norwich, Connecticut.

In 1948, these town meeting voters of Bridgewater, Vermont, considered whether to appropriate funds to help support a public health nurse. In 1987, the same town meeting voted on seven public welfare appropriations, ranging from programs for the elderly to a regional planning commission.

On Election Day in 1944, 68,000 citizens of Springfield, Massachusetts, went to the polls; in 1988, fewer than 47,000 voted.

Danbury, Connecticut

The annual Danbury Fair drew as many as 50,000 people a year in the 1880s. By 1901 railroads consigned special trains to the fairgrounds, and by 1941 attendance had reached 141,000, surpassing the state's six other agricultural fairs combined. For nine days each year, ox pulls competed with midget auto races, cattle judging with a three-ring circus, milking contests with the governor's annual fairgrounds visit.

That was in an era, however, when southern Fairfield County was still considered exurbia, and northern Fairfield — around Danbury — remained an area of working farms. But improved roads soon opened the Danbury area to suburban growth, and in time Danbury itself became a corporate headquarters city.

By then the Danbury Fair was an anachronism, a rural relic encircled by the footprints of the late twentieth century. In 1982, the fair closed forever, and four years later something new sprouted on the site: a 1,300,000-square-foot shopping mall containing 210 stores.

Amusement midway, Danbury Fair (above and facing page). A history of the fair described "a virtual city of paved expanses, modern exhibit buildings and midway attractions, which have contributed impressively to the entertainment and education of thousands."

Amusement midway, Danbury Fair. Friday was set aside as children's day at the fair in 1947. The previous year, for the first time in memory, the Danbury schools did not close at all during fair week, and a near-riot resulted.

Donald Ferris and his oxen, Danbury Fair. Ferris, of Newtown, Connecticut, competed in the fair's ox pull for sixty years. He won his last competition in 1978. When the mega-mall opened on the fairgrounds site eight years later, Ferris refused to visit it. "I had too much fun there," he said, "to see it now."

Gauthier Thibodeau (reading paper) arrived in Lancaster, New Hampshire, five years after he graduated from the University of Maine, to run the midpoint pumping station on Esso's Portland–Montreal pipeline. A year after this photograph was taken, he left his wife and family, moved to Venezuela, entered another marriage that would end in divorce, and eventually settled in Belfast, Maine, where he lives and works in one room above a barbershop.

The snowshoes bearing these pipeline maintenance workers in Lancaster have been replaced by snowmobiles. The original, 263-mile pipeline itself is now an electrical ground; a new line, double the capacity of the original, was laid alongside it in 1965.

This house was built by the artist Rockwell Kent long before telephone service came to Monhegan Island. Today the house is owned by Jamie Wyeth, a microwave system provides telephone communication to the mainland, and a proliferation of solar cell units have supplemented gasoline-powered generators that traditionally supplied the island with electrical power.

Herbert Allen's mixed herd of Holsteins, Ayrshires, Jerseys, and Guernseys, in West Springfield, Massachusetts, produced 400 quarts of milk daily in 1945. In time Allen gave up full-time dairying and worked as a milk inspector and then a hospital maintenance man.

The Allen Farm was one of nearly 6,500 Massachusetts dairy farms to disappear between 1940 and 1988, in this case because of high taxes. Fewer than 500 remain in operation today.

While in high school, Harry Haas worked as a farmhand for Herbert Allen. The land he is plowing is now a suburban housing development; Allen's son, John, still lives near the family farm, from which he commutes to the record store he owns in Springfield.

Eastern Point Light, Gloucester. The lighthouse is still functioning, but several large new houses have been built on the adjacent land.

Ed Townsend (center), Edgar Decker (front), and an unidentified fisherman on the deck of the *Eliza C. Riggs*. Townsend went to sea at fourteen and continued for at least thirty-six years, spending many of them in a drunken stupor. Decker was killed in a boat collision.

Gloucester, Massachusetts

The Gloucester of the 1940s was what it had been for three centuries — a city so tied to the sea that it wasn't easy to tell where city ended and sea began. Fishing vessels of various sizes lined the harbor for more than a mile, a floating community of men who spent more time at sea than ashore. The apparently limitless bounty of the ocean poured into Gloucester as if through a funnel. Along the waterfront, the frozen food industry — invented in Gloucester by a tinkerer named Clarence Birdseye in the 1920s — processed fish for a nation. In 1944, when Gordon Parks came to town, the lead story in the *Gloucester Daily News* was invariably about the war, the second lead about daily events in the fishing industry.

Fishing remains the largest employer in Gloucester, and the various waterfront enterprises still account for forty-five percent of the gross municipal product. Old shoreside offices bear signs advertising the services of lawyers specializing in admiralty work or immigration law (Portugal has replaced Italy as the largest source of new immigrants). But overfishing, competition from huge foreign trawlers, and outmoded technology have reduced the city's daily catch from a high of more than a million pounds a day to barely a tenth of that.

Captain Bill Lafond (with pipe)
and grandson Bill (in cap), Lafond's Wharf. The elder Lafond
began his life as a fisherman in
1897, when he was thirteen. His
grandson was still working on a
fishing boat eighty years later.

Aboard the *Riggs,* off Rockport.
Like most boats its size, the *Riggs*
had a crew of five — a captain, a
cook, and three hands. At virtually all times, three men would
be engaged in cleaning the
catch.

Joe Pallazola, aboard the *Rosie and Grace*. Pallazola seined for mackerel, traveling as far south as Virginia in pursuit of the fish and landing them in various ports along the way back to Gloucester. He dynamited his boat in the late sixties; it no longer had even scrap value.

David Maranhas, aboard the *Captain Dave*. Maranhas arrived in Gloucester from Portugal just before World War II, and soon established the Gloucester Oil Supply, scuttling about the harbor in his own boat to refuel the fleet. He owned and operated the business until just before his death in 1974, at the age of ninety-three.

Ellsworth Lafond, aboard the *Riggs*. Bill Lafond's son fished until his fifties, then took a job on land — delivering fish from a truck.

Gravestone, Good Harbor Cemetery. The man memorialized here with his daughter was fishing off Block Island when he pulled up a shark in his net. After killing the intruder with his double-barreled shotgun, he took a blast when the gun fired again. He bled to death in the arms of his brother.

Randy (left) and Ellsworth Lafond. Forty-two years after Gordon Parks took this picture, Ellsworth had been long dead, but Randy was still fishing. At eighty, he was working alone or with his wife, rather than pay $7,000 a year per crewman for insurance.

Almost all of the cotton mills —
more than a hundred of them —
that dominated Fall River, Massachusetts, were gone by 1953,
their functions transferred to the
south. Many of the old buildings
are now vast outlet stores for
companies that no longer manufacture in the city.

The Quonset area of Wickford,
Rhode Island, on Narragansett
Bay, was a resort district when
the government appropriated
the land for the Quonset Naval
Air Station during World War II.
The naval base is now an industrial park, the town itself a
suburb of Providence.

Before the advent of Lycra and Hollofil, skiwear in Stowe, Vermont, often consisted of the "mountain blankets" provided by the resort — heavy garments to be worn on the lifts, shed at the top of the trail, then (after being shipped back down by lift) donned again at the conclusion of a run.

The Mount Mansfield Hotel, nine miles from the center of Stowe, was built near the summit of Vermont's highest peak in 1858; it closed 100 years later and burned down 10 years after that.

Downtown Stowe is, virtually in its entirety, a registered historical district; each of the buildings in the picture is still standing. But today, a winter Saturday will draw as many as 10,000 cars to the village.

A Stowe laundry route, circa 1947: the V-shaped apparatus on the front of the sled served as a snowplow.

Jordan Marsh was at first dubious when invited to become the anchor tenant at Shoppers World, in Framingham, Massachusetts. The crowds Shoppers World drew, however, were so great that Jordan's parent company bought the entire mall within a year of its opening.

The idea of an enclosed mall was so new in 1951 that the primary lender, Equitable Life Insurance, required developer Houston Rawls to pay interest and amortization from the day the loan agreement was signed — a burden that led to Rawls's bankruptcy.

Somerville, Maine

The little settlement called Brown's Corner in the village of Somerville could have been the end of the earth in the early 1940s. It was really little more than the intersection of two dirt roads, with a few houses on one side of the intersection and a general store/gas station on the other. There was no telephone service in Brown's Corner, no electricity. The gasoline sold there came out of a hand-operated pump.

The hand that usually operated the pump belonged to Hercules Brown, who lived in one of the houses at Brown's Corner and operated the store, which his stepfather owned. Hercules was a man of little education, married to a woman who had come to town to teach in the one-room school. With their three daughters, they fashioned a life of sorts at their remote corner. But the apparently contented family enjoying dinner (with some neighboring children) in the picture on the opposite page struggled under the weight of Brown's alcohol problem. A former neighbor recalled that Brown, not having any liquor at hand, once drank twelve bottles of vanilla extract in one sitting.

(PRECEDING PAGE) **Dinner at Brown's Corner. Marion and Hercules Brown are in the foreground, their three daughters across the table (the girl to the immediate right of the kerosene lamp is a friend). During the war, two of the Brown girls worked in a plant that made shoes for the armed forces.**

Hercules Brown in his store. He operated the business for nearly forty years; he also served as the village postmaster.

Marion Brown. When her husband died in 1962, the store closed. She later moved in with one of her daughters, who ran a boarding house twenty minutes away, in Gardiner.

Marion Brown's father. Hercules's father and stepfather also lived in Brown's Corner. His natural father died a suicide, with the last words, "Poor Hercules, it'll be bad for Hercules."

The Brown store. Marion Brown is pumping gasoline for Larry French, a lumberman who lived nearby. The red oak is on its way to a Rockland shipyard that built minesweepers for the navy.

Harold French. One of Larry French's ten children, Harold helped out at the Browns' store. In the winter of 1944–45, the local school was closed because no teacher could be found.

The Chester–Hadlyme Ferry operates under a subsidy from the Connecticut Department of Transportation, mandated by the state legislature. It is, says a spokesman, "a tourist attraction."

Cutbacks in the naval presence in Newport, Rhode Island, led to tobacco heiress Doris Duke's expenditure of an estimated $10 million in restoration projects beginning in 1968. It is a measure of how dominant the Navy once was that, even today, it is the largest employer in Newport County and the second largest in the state.

By 1949 Camden, Maine, was already well into its conversion from a textile-mill town to a tourism center; today, the population of 4,500 doubles in the summer months.

Albert Thomas (facing page), his brother Said (above), and Albert's wife Bedrea operated their small market, in West Springfield, Massachusetts, for sixty-four years. Their lives were virtually circumscribed by one city block: both brothers and their families lived in a house directly behind the store.

The Thomas brothers (see previous page) drew most of their business from the Gilbert & Barker factory across the street. An Esso division that manufactured gas pumps, it was converted to defense work and staffed largely by women during World War II.

This Gilbert & Barker worker assembled torpedo guidance systems. Today, the G & B factory is operated by a smelting firm; the Thomas Brothers Market is a package liquor store.

The Sturbridge, Massachusetts, church auction, which was two years old when these photographs were taken in 1951, continued to thrive thirty-eight years later. What changed was the provenance of the goods for sale: in the early days, items were donated by townspeople, but as attics and cellars grew bare, the auction organizers began to purchase items at other auctions and donate them to the church.

Springfield, Massachusetts

Triangulating from what is generally known about the patterns of life in northeastern cities, one could come fairly close to learning the story of Springfield: sited on a major waterway (the Connecticut River), fueled in the nineteenth century by the dominance of one industry (arms manufacturing), attained its census peak in 1960 (174,000), then two-plus decades of population and economic decline.

In 1945, such an imminent downward slope was all but unimaginable. Springfield was then a city of 159,000, and a municipal authority was created to alleviate a severe housing shortage. A symphony orchestra had just been formed, and three locally owned department stores were thriving.

But soon one particular trend would bring a knife close to Springfield's heart: the decline of its downtown. Abetted by widespread car ownership, the atrophy of public transportation, the rise of suburban malls, and rapine urban renewal, the decline forever changed the way the city thought of itself. For those who had abandoned Springfield, it was more than a fair trade.

Neisner's, Main Street. This branch of the national chain disappeared in the early 1960s, its lot now occupied by a bank headquarters building.

David Rankin, Main and Bridge streets. The Springfield National Bank, across the street, became the Valley Bank following a merger, and was eventually swallowed by the Boston-based Bay Bank. The building, erected in 1887, has recently been renovated for office space.

Springfield Public Market, Main Street. This celebrated institution, from which a fleet of delivery trucks fanned out across the city every afternoon, closed in 1956, "an apparent victim of the shopping center boom," according to a news account. None of the nearby businesses survived into the 1960s, nor did the institution of the traffic officer in a booth.

Ryan Drug, Main and Cypress streets. Levelled in the urban renewal of the 1960s, Ryan Drug didn't become a self-service store until 1955, when it was sixty years old.

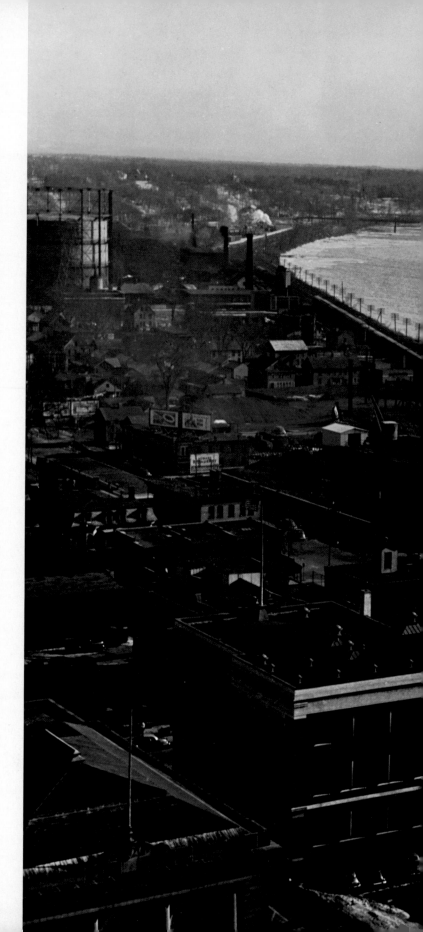

Reception, downtown Springfield. Guests at the premiere of *It Happened in Springfield* were celebrating the motion picture short made to popularize the Springfield Plan, a program promoting tolerance and civility in the city's school system. Much copied throughout the nation, the plan was abandoned in its native city by the early 1950s, when the city's demographic makeup began to change.

Facing south, downtown Springfield. However gritty the city's riverfront once was, at least the industry along the banks provided jobs. Today, the factories are gone, and the Connecticut River is no more accessible than it was — the entire near side of the riverfront has been given over to the speeding traffic of Interstate 91.

In 1951, when this cigar store Indian was on display at Old Sturbridge Village, attendance at the Massachusetts museum was 73,758. The Indian was removed from display in the 1950s, when Old Sturbridge decided to focus on the early American republic. In 1988, attendance reached 565,649.

Alfred Fuller began supplying his wares to independent salesmen, such as this resident of Monhegan Island, Maine, in the century's first decade. Today Fuller Brush is part of the Sara Lee Corporation, and methods have changed: the "Fuller Brush Man" is likely to be a woman, and door-to-door calls have been replaced by telemarketing.

Although Belgrade Depot, Maine, had telephone service as early as 1898, dial phones didn't come to the town until 1954.

Dr. Hans Loeffler (above, at right) owned this five-hundred-acre cattle farm in Monmouth, Maine, in the early 1940s. He also grew wheat, raised Berkshire pigs, and supplied the Navy with eggs. Since then, the farm has been reduced to thirty-five acres of mowed fields.

Bud Moore was four when he visited the South Deerfield, Massachusetts, farm of his Polish immigrant grandparents, Catie and Alex Bartos. After his family moved to Florida, Moore returned summers to help harvest potatoes, cucumbers, beets, and tobacco. Moore is an insurance agent in Hollywood, Florida.

Ice harvester, Waterford, Maine. In addition to the ice stored for local use, large quantities were also sent south via rail and ship. The industry began to disappear with the availability of electric refrigeration in the late 1940s.

The gasoline-driven ice cutter would first be used to cut a large sheet of ice several hundred feet square; thus circumscribed, the sheet rose on the water, to be cut up into 125- and 250-pound blocks.

Harrison, Maine, once the terminus of the Cumberland–Oxford Canal, a string of lakes connected by canal to Portland, was also a resort center whose hotels, cottages, and camps required large quantities of ice. The ice harvesting season generally began in December, and the blocks were stacked in sawdust in windowless buildings.

Northfield, Vermont

Rural free delivery, inaugurated on an experimental basis in West Virginia in 1896, was established as a permanent part of the American postal system in 1902. Dependent as it was on passable roads, the program also spurred one of the nation's first great highway building surges: between 1897 and 1908, an estimated $72 million was spent by local governments on bridges, culverts, levelings, and other improvements, as communities sought to bring their roads up to post office standards.

Charles Gilpin was one of the paladins of the RFD system. He began delivering mail around Northfield in 1928, when it cost two cents to send a first-class letter. His first few winters on the job, he traveled by horse-drawn sleigh, and before the holidays he would continue on his route each evening until everything had been delivered. "I saw him load up and go out on Christmas morning," one colleague recalled. "He wanted everyone to have their packages."

To supplement his income, Gilpin also farmed a small piece of land and helped out at his father's farm. He

put his two children through college, and he saved enough to retire early. But delivering the mail was something Gilpin loved to do, and he continued until his health would no longer allow it. Eventually, his body bent out of shape by forty years of lifting heavy bags and leaning across the front seat of his car, Gilpin retired, in 1968.

By then, mailing a first-class letter cost six cents.

Sorting the mail. In 1946, Gilpin's bag was regularly burdened by the Sears Roebuck catalog, the precursor of the mail order explosion that would occur in the late 1970s. The National Bulk Mail System was, by 1985, handling more than 32 billion pieces of bulk business mail a year.

At home. Gilpin's wife, Mary, is still living in Northfield; their son, Donald, became an accountant at the Columbus Zoo in Ohio; their daughter, Janice, became a registered nurse in Saint Albans, Vermont.

Donald and Charles Gilpin. The elder Gilpin was able to supplement his income by keeping a small herd of dairy cows, rising at 5:30 A.M. to do the milking before setting out on his postal rounds.

Selling a mail order. By dispensing money orders men like Gilpin brought a rudimentary banking system to Vermont's back roads. In 1946, the postal service sold nearly $5 billion in money orders. Forty years later, the spread of checking accounts had cut that figure nearly in half.

Billy Wise began coaching at Cathedral High, in Springfield, Massachusetts, in 1927 — the only layman on the faculty. His son, Billy, Jr., now the Cathedral football coach, is part of a faculty that is seventy percent laypeople.

The last of Vermont's five regional bookmobiles, similar to this one visiting the town of Duxbury, was taken out of service in 1974. Economy (the trucks got only five miles per gallon of gas) was one reason, but so was philosophy: the state felt the system isolated rural librarians, who now travel to regional centers to stock their collections. There are forty-nine towns in the state that do not have libraries.

The Oak Hill school, in Pownal, Vermont, is still owned by the local school district, but is used as a day-care center. In 1949, two years after this photograph was taken, the Green Mountain Race Track opened in Pownal — immediately becoming the largest tax supporter of the new, 366-student Pownal Elementary School, which replaced seven district schools like Oak Hill.

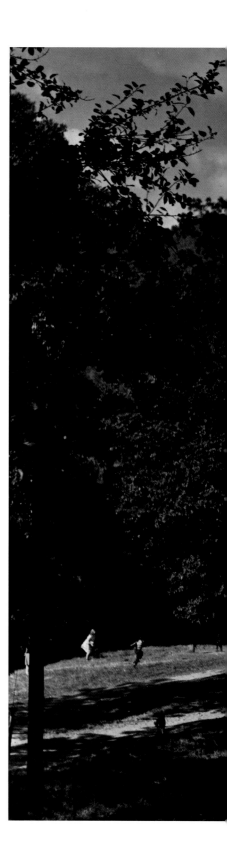

When World War II sent the three Wotowicz brothers, of Hadley, Massachusetts, into the Army and the Marines, their mother Honora (facing page, at left, weeding an onion field) and sister Josephine (with Honora) operated the family farm, growing tobacco, potatoes, feed corn, cabbage, and onions.

The Wotowicz house is still in the family, occupied by the widow of one of Josephine's brothers, but the farm itself is about to be converted into a golf course.

In addition to her farm labors, Josephine Wotowicz also worked an eight-hour shift in a defense plant. She later married a neighboring farmer and worked in the infirmary at the University of Massachusetts in Amherst until her retirement in 1975.

Everett, Massachusetts

"The curling smoke from the factory chimneys and the screaming whistle calling to services," a local historian wrote in 1910, "stamps our city as an industrial center, with men and women of all races and classes. . . ." The Colonial Beacon Oil Co. — later part of Esso — joined the industrial throng outside Boston on the banks of the Mystic River in 1919, building the only refinery in New England. Its neighbors eventually would include a Monsanto factory, the Boston Edison generating plant, the New England Coke Works, and the General Electric supercharger division.

Esso attempted to foster a family feeling at its plant. Fearing the incursions of the CIO, the company paid better than other oil companies, matched employee savings up to ten percent of an employee's pay, and provided regular, on-site medical examinations. Still, when the Everett refinery ceased being economical, Esso closed it down.

The city, though, barely noticed. By 1965, an industrial presence was no longer anything that small cities bragged about.

Gas still. At its peak, the refinery employed more than 1,000 people. Before it closed, the staff had already shrunk to less than 300.

Refinery lab. Twenty-four hours a day, shifting groups of technicians — usually women — took regular readings on the refinery's output, testing the viscosity of oil and gasoline.

Clinic. Staff nurse Kay Kaspar arrived at the Everett Refinery in 1941 and stayed nearly a quarter-century, until the facility was closed down. Most staff members were offered jobs at other Esso facilities; one recalled being asked to choose among Bayonne, New Jersey; Baton Rouge, Louisiana; and the Caribbean island of Aruba. Kaspar decided to stay in Everett.

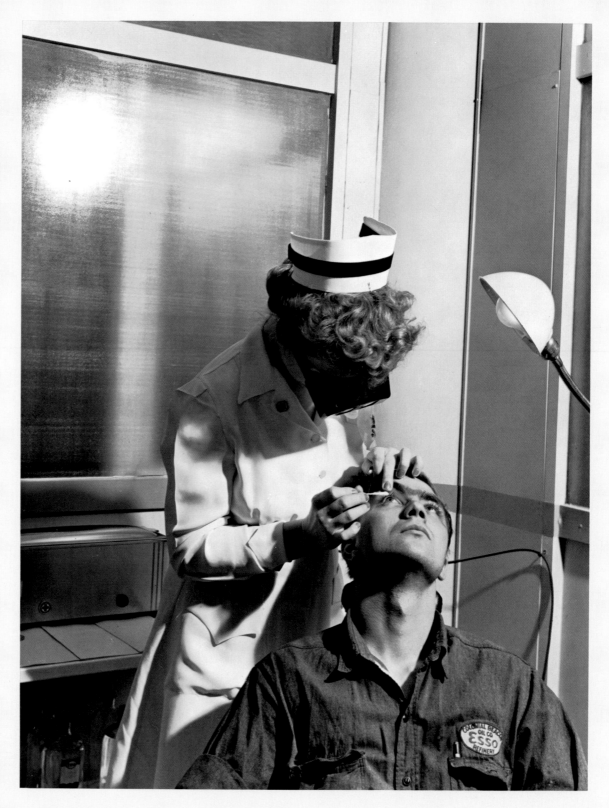

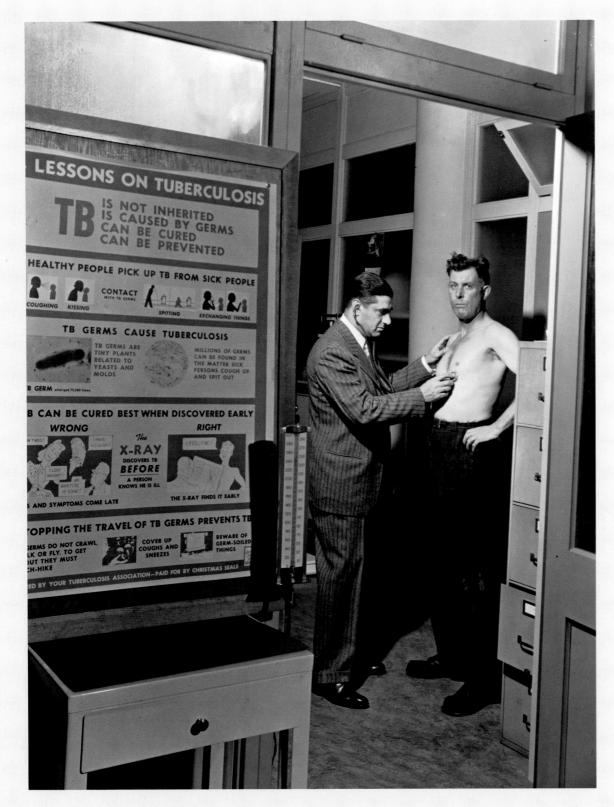

Dr. Charles Barbarisi. The doctor was on retainer to Esso, and his primary concern was tuberculosis. In 1946, just before the advent of modern milk production, TB was nearly ten times as common in Massachusetts as it was in the late 1980s.

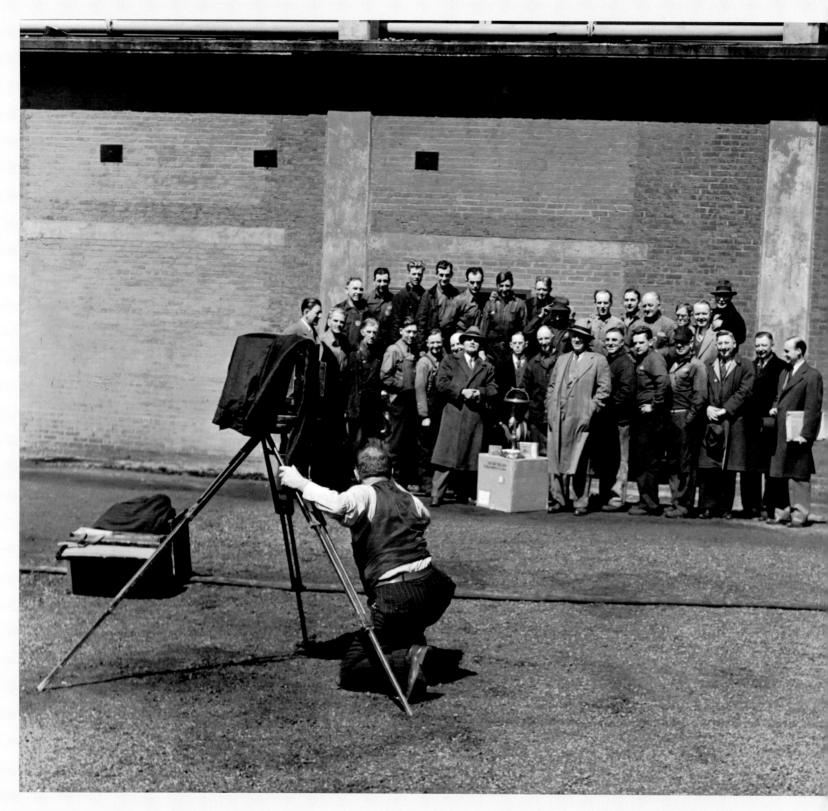

Pete McCauley. McCauley, who
was born in Ireland, was an Esso
welder for more than twenty
years. Like other employees, he
belonged to the independent
union organized by manage-
ment in its successful effort to
keep away more militant unions.

Retirement party. Joseph
Murphy (extreme left, front row)
managed the Esso refinery. Photographer Gus Braun was an Everett fixture who traveled from
factory to schoolhouse, record-
ing events exactly like this one.

122 THE WAY WE WERE

When photographed in 1946, this school, in East Roxbury, Vermont, was one of hundreds of one-room schoolhouses in the state. Today only five remain in operation. State-certification plates, such as the one near the window of this building, were made in state prisons and are now prized by antiques collectors.

Maine, too, has witnessed the near-extinction of one-room schoolhouses, the successors of the original "Dame Schools" operated, as one history has it, "by some kindly spinster or resolute housewife." This one, in Bridgeton, was replaced in the 1960s by a central elementary school and a consolidated high school serving four towns. Between 1940 and 1963, annual per pupil expenditures in Bridgeton increased eightfold.

This stretch of the Connecticut River Valley in western Massachusetts, viewed here from Mount Sugarloaf in South Deerfield, remained unsullied until 1967, when the extension of I-91 bisected it. The forty-eight miles of the highway in Massachusetts took eleven years to build, at a cost of $180 million.

The shortage of consumer goods during World War II made the war years the most profitable that Bart Morrill, of Bradford, Vermont, would ever know. Forty-one years after this photograph was taken, his son acknowledged that competition had forced Gove & Morrill to become "a paint store that happens to sell hardware."

World War II's labor shortages and food rationing helped the small farmer nearly as much as the Farm Security agency had a decade earlier. This farm stand near Augusta, Maine, provided a meaningful supplement to its operator's income that would all but disappear with the war's end and the advent of new systems of food distribution.

During the war, intercity rail travel reached its all-time peak; gas rationing kept stations such as the Boston & Albany depot, in Springfield, Massachusetts, busy twenty-four hours a day.

The Springfield station isn't nearly as important a travel hub as it was in 1945, but it is serving more passengers than it has in decades. Since 1972, passenger mileage logged on Amtrak lines has nearly doubled.

Skowhegan, Maine

Sylvester and Janie Moore. He was, neighbors remember, "a good Christian who didn't have much use for church." Janie, on the other hand, was a devoted Baptist who struggled with Sylvester's habit of tippling from a bottle he hid in a cupboard.

Turney Moore. After he inherited his father's farm, Turney had to struggle to keep it solvent. When it became clear that his only son, John, did not want the land, Turney sold it off piecemeal and engaged in twenty separate land transactions in one five-year period.

There were three Skowhegans in the 1940s: the farming community, the community in town, and the community of the lumber camps. The first was largely of English or Scottish stock, the second was similar although it included an admixture of Jewish shop owners, and the third was mostly French Canadian. "The fields and town belonged to us," one Anglophone said in 1987, "and the woods belonged to them." The French reached Skowhegan along the old Kennebec–Chaudiere trail, a forest path that predated a highway that now runs to Jackman.

But even the two English-speaking communities were divided. The farm people generally went into town as little as possible, and except for the occasional teenager trying to earn extra money as a part-time farmhand, the townspeople never went to the farms. For people like Sylvester Moore and his wife, existing as they did in a cash-only, debt-free economy, the town of Skowhegan was something generally to be dealt with only when there was a will to be filed, or a deed to sign.

Paul Blake and his son Robert. Paul was the Moores' hired man from 1942 until 1945, terminating his arrangement — a small house, fresh milk, and a few dollars a week — on VJ Day. He later worked as a sawmill manager. His son has been an auditor at a shoe factory for the last twenty-four years.

Paul Blake. He and Turney Moore "worked hard enough on that farm to earn two or three army deferments," he remembered. Sylvester Moore was one of the last farmers in Skowhegan to convert entirely to power machinery. The horses here were named May and June.

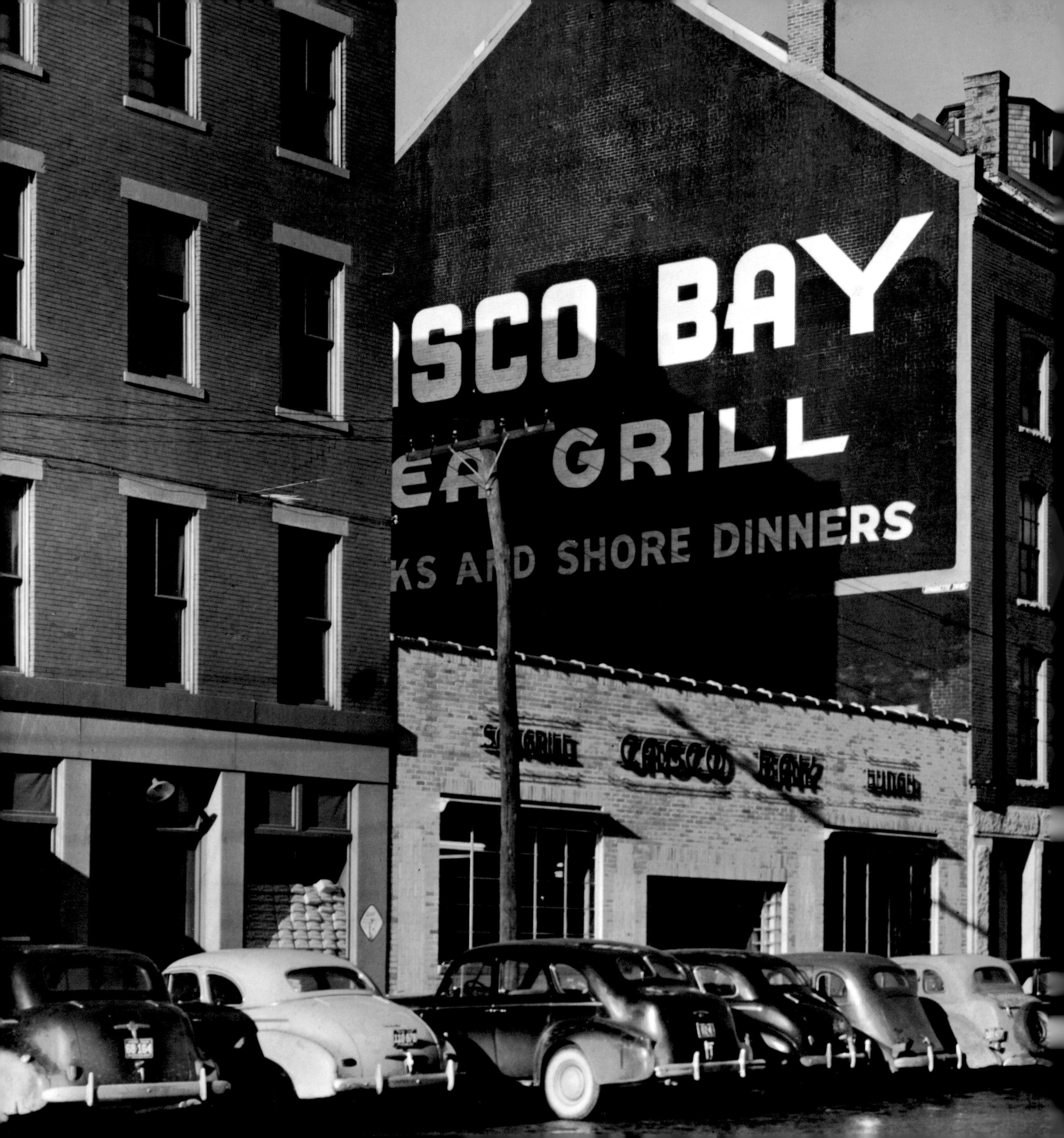
SCO BAY
EA GRILL
KS AND SHORE DINNERS

A ten-story office and parking complex has risen directly behind this block on Commercial Street, in Portland, Maine. The Casco Bay Sea Grill has been replaced by a computer sales firm, and the wall that bore the grill's sign has been perforated by a large Palladian window.

Regular ferry service between Jamestown and Newport, Rhode Island, began in 1675 and ended in 1969 with the opening of the Newport Bridge. The steamer here, the *Governor Carr,* could carry forty cars and five hundred passengers at a time.

This intercity contest, in Springfield, Massachusetts, was a herald of the coming boom in amateur softball; today, a 240-team adult league operates in the city's parks. At the professional level, though, Springfield lost its last minor league team in 1965.

East Orange, Vermont

George Richardson, Harold's father, was a farmer and the tax collector for the town of Corinth. He named his prize oxen Scotch and Soda.

Ada and Harold Richardson. Both Richardsons are dead now. Their daughter, Herma, lives in West Topsham, Vermont; their son, Kermit, is a member of the Vermont legislature.

Harold and Ada Richardson bought their small grocery and general store in the 1920s and ran it together until Harold's death in 1955. It was characteristic of a Vermont village store, a compact emporium whose size belied the wealth of goods on its shelves, where barter was as common as cash transactions. The Richardsons stocked molasses and vinegar in barrels, animal hides, feed, and candy. They purchased their packaged goods through Nationwide Service Grocers, a national buying cooperative of independent store owners.

Such was the role of the shop in a place like East Orange that it was as much social service center as retail establishment. For three years in the early 1950s, twenty-two students from the town's one-room schoolhouse would run down the street at noon and climb the stairs inside the Richardson store for the hot lunches that Ada prepared each day. The PTA and other civic groups had their meetings in the same upstairs room.

In 1985, the old Richardson store was torn down, and a house was built in its place.

Lunch line at the Richardson store. At the rear of the line is Lettie O'Meara, the school-teacher, who began teaching in one-room schoolhouses in the East Orange area when she was a teenager.

Lunchtime. Flora Gray (left) and several of her siblings all left East Orange when they completed the eighth grade — the closest high school was a five-mile walk distant. They attended high school in Connecticut, where they lived with an older sister.

Hutchinson family arriving for a PTA dinner. Delmar Hutchinson owned and operated a farm in the town of Washington for fifty-two years; he and his wife, Arlene (left), still live there. All five of their children (the youngest is forty) live within an hour's drive of East Orange.

PTA dinner. Delmar Hutchinson
is reaching across the table; the
man next to him is Leo Butler, a
local farmer and woodcutter.

Ada Richardson. For the daily school lunches — the ingredients, the cooking, the cleaning up — Mrs. Richardson was paid thirty cents a head.

Returning to school after lunch. The school, just this side of the church, is now used as a storage building. The church itself, which celebrates its centennial in 1990, is being renovated by Delmar Hutchinson's sons, Delmar, Jr., and Jay (the young boy in the photograph on page 142).

Springfield, Massachusetts, inaugurated summer Pops concerts in 1944, in the city's Museum Quadrangle. Admission was free, and chairs were rented for fifteen cents each.

The Springfield Pops concerts continue today in Forest Park, but competition from various forms of entertainment have cut attendance from the highs — as many as five thousand people at a single concert — reached in the forties.

W. R. Cutter was a prosperous tobacco farmer in East Hatfield, Massachusetts, who over time sold off pieces of his land for other purposes — a Howard Johnson's was built on one parcel, a driving range on another. Although he sold the last of his land in 1952, a year before he died, a grandson, a great-grandson, and a great-great-grandson still live in East Hatfield.

Amede Thibault worked the lumber camps of Vermont in the 1940s, including this one near Bridgewater Corners. He was part of a shifting crowd of wood-cutters, mostly French Cana-dian, who eventually would be replaced by machines operated by local residents. Despite the sharp drop in employment fig-ures, the industry's volume has never been higher than it is now; 333,000 cords of pulpwood and 207 million board feet of lumber were harvested in Vermont in 1987.

Ed Parkhurst operated his own grocery store/gas station in Unity, Maine, until the early 1960s, when he sold it after suffering a stroke. The building is now owned by a health food cooperative.

The land Joe Yarrows once farmed with his family in Hadley, Massachusetts, is now divided into house lots and a Christmas tree farm.

A speed limit of fifty miles per hour in daylight, thirty-five after dark, was all that impeded travelers on Route 6, the major link between Hartford and Providence. Few were aware that during the war, from a secret installation along the roadside, government employees triangulated tank positions in North Africa.

More than 3,800,000 cars traveled on the Maine Turnpike in 1955, the year it opened. Thirty years later, the number had increased to more than 31,000,000 — about half of them from out of state.

Williamstown, Massachusetts, was the site of Williams College and of the homes of the industrial oligarchs of nearby North Adams. But after the mills and factories of the latter city emptied in the 1950s and 1960s, many of Williamstown's grand mansions were converted into inns or transformed into weekend houses for vacationing New Yorkers.

Hanover,
New Hampshire

In the years immediately after World War II, Dartmouth College — like most New England colleges — bore little relation to what it was before the war, or what it would become several years later. In 1947, it was all-male (as it would remain for nearly three more decades), but the return of older servicemen — fifty-eight undergraduates became fathers during the 1947–48 academic year — radically affected the nature of campus life.

On an intellectual plane, the returning veterans were concerned with the shape of the postwar world. Campus debates revolved around various One World plans, the partition of Palestine, and other Great Issues, as they were called in a course conducted for the entire senior class. Speakers included George Kennan, Reinhold Niebuhr, Sidney Hook, and a young California congressman who, *The Daily Dartmouth* said, "completely buffaloed the Great Issues course with his slick, tough-guy tactics. Five hundred seniors sat like dumb lumps as the congressman [Richard M. Nixon] went through his renowned cloak-and-dagger histrionics. . . ."

(PRECEDING PAGE) Robert Frost. At Dartmouth, where nothing gets thrown out, the chair Frost occupied during his poetry class and the lamp that illuminated his brow are still in the same room, in roughly the same places. The seventh student from the left, Russell Blackwood, became a professor at Hamilton College.

Richardson Hall. Now a coeducational dormitory (as are all of Dartmouth's dorms), Richardson in 1947 accommodated eighty-eight students in its thirty-eight rooms. Room charges for the academic year ranged from $150 to $220 for a ground-floor single.

Classroom. The war veterans brought a certain seriousness to Hanover, but the maleness of the place still manifested itself on social weekends. Before one such weekend in the spring of 1948, a *Daily Dartmouth* headline reported "Girls from 48 States, 75 Colleges Come by Air, B&M, Car in Skirted Invasion."

"Hums." The annual singing event was falling into postwar disfavor, but Dartmouth's Outing Club had 850 members, out of a 1948 enrollment of 2,083. In a straw poll, those 2,083 divided seventy-seven percent for Thomas Dewey, thirteen percent for Harry Truman, and seven percent for Henry Wallace.

The presence of railroad stops — first the Connecticut & Passumpsic, then the Boston & Maine, finally the Canadian Pacific — brought prosperity to Lyndonville, Vermont; when the railroads began to leave, after a strike in 1922, so did much of the town's wealth. This grand house still stands, but by 1987 the elm tree was gone, and a derelict school bus was sitting in the driveway.

Each year on Washington's Birthday, Lyndonville residents staged sleigh races on an iced-over Main Street. But the buggy in the foreground was not built for racing; like many other carriages in the area, it was made from an automobile chassis better suited than a wooden wagon for the area's hard, bumpy roads.

Earl Clark (at right) worked as an accountant until his wife inherited Libby Bros., in Albion, Maine, in the 1920s. He sold groceries, feed, and Esso gasoline, delivered the groceries free throughout the area, and owned the town's first television set. Libby Bros. is now a convenience store and coffee shop.

Colonial Beacon was an oil products wholesaler whose trucks were nearly ubiquitous in greater Boston. Here, in Belmont, Massachusetts, a delivery is made to a home last sold, in 1971, for $55,000; today, its market value is estimated at $750,000.

Colonial's gasoline enterprise extended to this solitary service station, in Stowe, Vermont, shown here in 1947. Two years earlier, the American automobile industry resumed production after a three-year hiatus. At the time, barely fifty percent of American households owned cars.

The Curtis Hotel, in Lenox, Massachusetts, at left in the photograph, was once the sort of hostelry that accommodated summer vacationers who would stay for weeks at a time, people who came to Lenox for "the season." Its upper floors later were remodeled into housing for the elderly, its street-level space a gallery of specialty shops.

West Suffield, Connecticut

Horse team. The use of horses for farm work in Connecticut all but ended with the increased manufacture of farm equipment in the postwar years.

Herbert Anderson. A Jamaican, he worked on Consolidated Cigar's Bissell Farm, in West Suffield.

The tobacco farmers of the Connecticut River Valley had names as grand as their holdings — Imperial Tobacco, American Sumatra, General Cigar. During the war, when severe labor shortages compelled the growers to replace local laborers, they relied on two unlikely sources: West Indians "loaned" to the U.S. by Winston Churchill, and (during the harvest) teenage girls imported from throughout the northeast.

In the town of Suffield, the West Indians found a relatively hospitable environment. The town had had a black church since 1903, and a black resident, Gordon Hayes, was appointed to the police force in 1941. On the tobacco farms, the imported laborers saved as much as $12.50 a week after room and board, most of it paid directly into government-managed escrow accounts in the islands.

When the wartime labor shortages were over, most of the West Indians returned home, but several hundred — most of them having married American citizens — stayed in Connecticut.

Tobacco nets. For decades a familiar sight in the Connecticut Valley between Hartford and the Massachusetts–Vermont border, the nets that shielded tobacco leaf from the sun now cover less than ten percent of the acreage they protected in the early 1950s.

Geneva Hudley. Hudley was a member of one of the two primary classes of female labor — local high school girls and farm girls brought in from elsewhere. The largest contingent of the latter were from Pennsylvania and were known throughout the area as "Pennsy Girls."

Frank Bergh. Bergh was superintendent of the Bissell Farm, which is now the property of a wholesale nursery farm. The fields where the tobacco nets once stood harbor row after row of flowering plum trees.

Feed store. Suffield still has some farms within its borders, but it is now mostly a commuter suburb of Hartford, its Main Street a near-museum-quality collection of expensive clapboard homes.

Jamaican workers, Bissell Farm. A few camps remain in operation in the Connecticut Valley today, and Jamaica is still a major source for seasonal laborers.

The feed business of E. T. & H. K. Ide has been in the same family since 1813 and has operated at this site (now a depot on the Canadian Pacific line) in St. Johnsbury, Vermont, since 1879.

In 1945, the Canadian Pacific, here entering the United States near North Troy, Vermont, supplied New England industries. Canadian Pacific gave up the last of its steam locomotives in 1949.

In 1944, Maine's Windsor County Fair was fifty-six years old. A centennial history published in 1988 asserted that "Windsor Fair has always tried to maintain a proper balance between vegetables, animals, midway and horse racing, fancy goods, food and fun."

The presence of uniformed servicemen was not the only sign of wartime at the fair in the early 1940s: the fair itself had been closed in 1942 and 1943 because of federal restrictions. In 1943, the fair's trustees issued a statement explaining why the event "could not or should not be held this year."

In 1944, the trustees paid $1,250 to secure the services of two vaudeville troupes, the Molly York Show and the Ray Flanders Show. Although the ox pull was still one of the most popular events at the time, by 1979 it had been supplanted to large degree by tractor and four-wheel-drive truck pulls.

In 1947, the woolen mills of Woonsocket, Rhode Island, were still flush from the large profits they had gathered milling fabrics for the government during the war. Within ten years, they had followed the cotton mills south to less unionized locales.

A few miles away, in Pawtucket, the jewelry industry survived as the textile industry did not. By 1947, this factory had been making "findings" — the various small clasps, hooks, connecting rings, and such that comprise functional jewelry parts — for nearly one hundred years. Today eighty percent of American-made jewelry is still fabricated in the Providence-Pawtucket area.

The first tractor on Joe Yarrows's farm, in Hadley, Massachusetts (see page 149), didn't arrive until 1950. Joe Moody, the farmhand in this picture, used this team of horses to cultivate the farm's asparagus beds. He later became a salesman.

Joe Yarrows, Jr., worked as a lathe operator on an evening shift, and spent mornings and Sundays helping his aging father on the family farm. The town in which it was located, part of what was once known as The Asparagus Valley, is now dominated by two huge malls. The older one, built less than twenty years ago, is now all but empty; the newer one, right next door, is filled with the stores that once occupied its ghostly neighbor.

Credits

FRONTISPIECE: Gordon Parks, August 1944

PAGE VI: Esther Bubley, July 1944

PAGE 2: Gordon Parks, August 1944

PAGE 2: Gordon Parks, August 1944

PAGE 36: Charlotte Brooks, October 1944

PAGE 37: Charlotte Brooks, October 1946

PAGE 38: Todd Webb, January 1947

PAGE 39: Todd Webb, October 1947

PAGES 40–41: Todd Webb, September 1947

PAGE 42: Todd Webb, October 1947

PAGE 43: Gordon Parks, February 1945

PAGE 44: Gordon Parks, October 1947

PAGE 45: Gordon Parks, October 1947

PAGE 46: Arnold Eagle, August 1949

PAGE 47: Gordon Parks, October 1947

PAGES 48–49: Gordon Parks, September 1947

PAGE 50 (BOTH): Todd Webb, February 1949

PAGE 51: Gordon Parks, May 1945

PAGE 52: Todd Webb, October 1947

PAGE 53: Todd Webb, October 1947

PAGE 54: Charlotte Brooks, March 1946

PAGE 55: Gordon Parks, July 1944

PAGE 56: Sol Libsohn, October 1947

PAGE 57: Sol Libsohn, October 1947

PAGE 58: Sol Libsohn, October 1947

PAGE 59: Sol Libsohn, October 1947

PAGE 60: John Vachon, February 1945

PAGE 61: John Vachon, February 1945

PAGE 62: Arnold Eagle, August 1951

PAGE 63: Gordon Parks, May 1945

PAGE 64: Gordon Parks, May 1945

PAGE 65: Gordon Parks, July 1945

PAGE 66: Gordon Parks, November 1944

PAGE 67: Gordon Parks, November 1944

PAGE 68: Gordon Parks, November 1944

PAGE 69: Gordon Parks, November 1944

PAGE 70: Gordon Parks, December 1944

PAGE 71 (GAS PUMPER): Gordon Parks, January 1945

PAGE 71 (MAN WITH PIPE): Gordon Parks, November 1944

PAGE 72: Gordon Parks, January 1945

PAGE 73: Gordon Parks, January 1945

PAGE 74: Todd Webb, October 1947

PAGE 75: Gordon Parks, September 1947

PAGE 76 (BOTH): Arnold Eagle, March 1947

PAGE 77 (MAIN STREET): Charlotte Brooks, February 1946

PAGE 77 (MAN PULLING SLED): Arnold Eagle, March 1947

PAGE 78: Diane Witlin, October 1951

PAGE 79: Diane Witlin, October 1951

PAGES 80–81: Gordon Parks, February 1944

PAGE 82 (BOTH): Gordon Parks, February 1944

PAGE 83: Gordon Parks, February 1944

PAGE 84: Gordon Parks, February 1944

PAGE 85: Gordon Parks, February 1944

PAGE 86: Charlotte Brooks, September 1946

PAGE 87 (NEWPORT): Arnold Eagle, September 1954

PAGE 87 (CAMDEN): Arnold Eagle, August 1949

PAGE 88: Esther Bubley, July 1944

PAGE 89: Esther Bubley, July 1944

PAGE 90: Esther Bubley, July 1944

PAGE 91: Esther Bubley, July 1944

PAGE 92: Esther Bubley, August 1951

PAGE 93: Esther Bubley, August 1951

PAGE 94: Gordon Parks, February 1945

PAGE 95: Gordon Parks, February 1945

PAGE 96: Gordon Parks, February 1945

PAGE 97: Gordon Parks, May 1945

PAGE 98: Gordon Parks, May 1945

PAGE 99: Gordon Parks, February 1945

PAGE 100 (TELEPHONE): Gordon Parks, February 1944

PAGE 100 (CIGAR STORE INDIAN): Esther Bubley, August 1951

PAGE 101: Arnold Eagle, August 1951

PAGE 102: Gordon Parks, August 1944

PAGE 103: Gordon Parks, October 1947

PAGE 104 (BOTH): John Vachon, February 1945

PAGE 105: John Vachon, February 1945

PAGE 106: Charlotte Brooks, October 1946

PAGE 107: Charlotte Brooks, October 1946

PAGE 108: Charlotte Brooks, October 1946

Designed by Impress

Art direction by Michael Grinley

The Way We Were

was printed on Lithofect Plus Dull

by Rembrandt Press

Composed in Compugraphic Bembo

by Walker Rumble

with display type in Kennerley

Bound by Nicholstone Book Bindery